Church Discipline

God's Gift for a Healthier, Holier Church

James T. South

Church Discipline: God's Gift for a Healthier, Holier Church
© 2015 by James T. South
P.O. Box 6259, Chillicothe, Ohio 45601
800.300.9778
www.deward.com

Cover design by Eric Wallace.

Printed in the United States of America.

ISBN: 978-1-936341-74-0

With affection and gratitude, this book is dedicated to the members of the *Glen Allen Church of Christ*, who love to hear the word, and who are a constant encouragement to me in the preaching of it.

Foreword

"I could believe in Jesus if only he did not drag behind Him his lep-rous bride, the church." Those words, in one form or another, have been attributed to several 19th century authors, including Southey, Shelly, and Swinborne; but they are unhappily contemporary. One modern mantra runs, "Jesus, yes; the church, no." Most people who know something about Jesus find Him attractive, but many unbelievers find the empirical church, the church they see, either repulsive or irrelevant, and even some believers find it unsatisfy-ing, even irritating at times. This deplorable situation yields much bitter fruit. What are we to make of this disjunction between an attractive Jesus and His perceived "leprous bride"?

Of course, all individual churches are not leprous. I am grate-ful for those that have nurtured and encouraged me in righteous-ness. I know many others who share this view. Nevertheless, a broad spectrum of people in our society does not find church life satisfying or fulfilling, not even attractive. Somehow people feel in their bones that churches should have credibility and integrity. After all, isn't that the way they portray themselves? Leaders in each church must face this situation and engage in serious self-analysis. Both church effectiveness and church incompetence are complex matters for those who want to be analytical, but much of it has to do with the integrity of discipleship. People can be happy with a church without realizing that it is failing in some of its intended purposes, that it serves as a kind of spiritual palliative that neglects the character-building purposes of the church. So, what can be done about it?

Dr. Tommy South has tackled this condition through his valuable study of the two-pronged nature of church discipline. True, church discipline is not the single answer to the dilemma faced in North America, but it deals significantly with the integrity of church membership, the validity of being disciples of Jesus. It cheers my heart to contemplate the difference it would make if the truth found in his book would be heeded.

The very mention of church discipline in the USA runs counter to several prominent cultural values in our country: individual freedom ("to do as I please"), pronounced individualism that avoids community responsibility, and a pluralism that worships tolerance and eschews most insistence on standards. Parallel to these forces is the tendency by some churches to accommodate themselves unhealthily to the culture, hoping thereby to grow larger. It is ironic that in many cases the very efforts exerted to make the church grow larger serve to minimize its use of developmental and corrective discipline. Albert Mohler is quoted as saying, "Put simply, the abandonment of church discipline is linked to American Christianity's creeping accommodation to American culture." To practice such discipline appears to be an uphill battle. Church discipline, however, is a solid New Testament teaching in multiple texts, and for that reason Christian leaders throughout history have recognized its place in being faithful to God. Cyprian, John Chrysostom, the Anabaptists, Calvin, Luther and many others to our own day have advocated church discipline. I have read a number of books on the subject written by fellow members of churches of Christ, but none as full and satisfying to me as Dr. South's treatment of the subject.

The initial exegetical basis for this study was Dr. South's doctoral dissertation on the discipline texts in the Pauline epistles. For that, however, the book is not burdened with technical matters. The benefits from the dissertation are retained without inflicting upon the reader academic jargon and multiple references to technical word studies, articles, and commentaries. Already in the first edition of this work (*That We May Share His Holiness*, 1997) Dr. South expanded his consideration of the subject beyond the Pauline texts to include passages in Matthew, Hebrews and 3 John. This new edition contains two entire chapters on Matthew 18.

In addition to his biblical scholarship, however, Dr. South brings to this subject extensive ministry experience in the local church. He has preached/taught for many years and also served as a shepherd (pastor)/elder/overseer—all levels of ministry at which leadership in church discipline takes place. He has dealt with some of the hard, practical issues about which he writes. For a long time he has had interest in evangelizing, at home and abroad. When one church with which he worked sponsored a couple to work among the Navajo, Dr. South called weekly to give encouragement. He and I have taught together in Seoul, South Korea. The church he now serves is engaged in an ongoing effort to plant and nurture a church in Western Ukraine. At the same time, he teaches Early Christianity in a metropolitan University. This book is a happy display of scholarship in practical service to the church.

Dr. South knows first-hand the price paid for the two extreme responses to the church discipline texts: complete neglect and avoidance, on the one hand, and heavy-handed, vindictive, unloving discipline on the other. He knows both the complexity and benefits of applying discipline. Here one reads from a practitioner, not a theoretician. In his life of ministry he has seen many cases of churches that specialize in saying, "Everyone is welcome" or

"Make this your church home" while having very porous boundaries and a terribly shallow understanding of fellowship. That is one reason South gives serious attention to the nature of fellowship and "boundary maintenance." A significant part of the practical nature of the book is found in the useful cases-in-point, descriptions of real persons and churches that illustrate the good and bad practices with which South deals exegetically.

While churches may be urged by *leaders* to engage in discipline, it is the *church itself* that carries out the discipline. The decision to practice or neglect it must take into consideration the way it touches a number of matters fundamental to faithfulness: the nature of the church, the integrity of church membership, the development of holiness, the vitality of fellowship, and the rescue of those who have been overtaken by sin or have deliberately turned to a destructive path. In church discipline leaders and congregations come face to face with the meaning of responsible love.

C. Philip Slate, D. Miss.

Retired professor, author of *Handbook on Missions for Local Churches*, *Perspectives on Worldwide Evangelization*, and (with Stan Granberg) *Reaching "Russia."*

Contents

Author's Preface

It has now been almost eighteen years since the publication of *That We May Share His Holiness: A Fresh Approach to Church Discipline* (Abilene, Texas: Bible Guides, 1997). My dear friend and teacher Neil Lightfoot generously offered to publish it after reading the manuscript, because he believed it to be an important study of a long-neglected topic. In the intervening years the book has had an interesting history. It was favorably reviewed in several publications and led to the opportunity to teach on church discipline at lectureships and workshops in various places. Several years ago, realizing that we had some unsold copies left, Neil encouraged me to make the remaining books available free of charge to ministers, elders, missionaries, and others who were interested in reading it. As a result the book has now been read in various places around the world and has had more influence in the past few years than in the first decade after its publication. I am especially indebted to Dr. C. Philip Slate for much of this outcome, since he has carried copies with him on travels around the world and distributed them to those who promised to read them.

This renewed interest in my book and in the subject of church discipline itself causes me to think it is time for a complete revision. There are several reasons for this. One is the amount of new material I have developed or become aware of over the past seventeen years. Somewhat surprisingly, there are still not many published works on the subject of church discipline, but there have been a few noteworthy additions to the literature,[1] and I want to make readers aware of them, as well as add new material that I have developed for presentation in workshops with church leaders both in the U.S. and abroad. Much of this new material is intended specifically for elders, who are, in my opinion, the key to whether or not discipline takes place within a church but who often feel inadequate for the task or are not clear what the task involves. Part of the need for such an approach stems from the fact that, while numerous good studies of the role of elders as shepherds have appeared in recent years along with books on why people fall away and what can be done to restore them, almost never do these mention the disciplinary aspects of the shepherd's role, which seems to me a curious, if not a tragic, omission.

An interesting development in the study of church discipline over the past seventeen years is the amount of material now available on the Internet. There are numerous articles, blogs, church policy statements, and other documents, many of which have some value.[2] However, there are still very few book-length studies, and almost none which focus primarily on the New Testament texts as providing the basis and appropriate guidelines for discipline. In addition, much of the available material is colored by the church affiliations of the authors, which makes it of limited value to those who don't share their views of church organization and/or practices. While it's encouraging to see a renewed interest in discipline,

---

[1] In addition to works specifically on the subject of discipline, some of the best information is found in several of the more recent commentaries on the various books which contain texts on discipline. Some of these are cited in the following chapters. It is especially gratifying to see that my academic research on 1 Corinthians 5, published more than two decades ago, has begun to influence the thinking of the authors of several of these commentaries.

[2] For a sampling, see the articles available at www.monergism.com/search?keywords=church+discipline&format=All.

as evidenced by so many online publications promoting its practice, there is still a void where in-depth study of the biblical texts is concerned. It is that void I hope to at least partially fill in this book.

Therefore, one thing that has not changed about this new edition is the focus on the specific Scripture texts which speak of discipline. This is, and in my opinion must always be, the heart of all our discussions about discipline. Although I have completely re-written these sections, the substance of them remains basically the same, since I believe my exegesis of the selected texts remains sound. This does not by any means suggest that my conclusions are unassailable but only that the ground has been adequately covered to discover what the Spirit continues to say to the churches.[3] As a result of the continuation of this exegetical approach, the reader will find here the same emphasis as in the earlier version, that the practice of discipline arises out of a deep awareness of the holiness of God and of the holiness He desires for His people. The need for discipline is not rooted simply in a number of scattered texts which teach it; rather it is rooted in the necessity for God's people to become like Him and to deal lovingly but decisively with those who refuse to do so. Likewise, we must learn to think of discipline not as a burden but as a gift. Church life never is, and never has been, perfect. Situations often arise that are extremely difficult, and discipline is a God-given means of dealing with some of the most troubling and disruptive ones.

A few explanations: Some reviewers of the original book wondered why some texts which they regard as disciplinary in nature were not discussed and why there was not more emphasis on "church discipline" in the broader sense of everything that goes into making disciples (sometimes referred to as "positive disci-

---

[3]For the more technical issues concerning the Pauline texts, see the various commentaries cited in later chapters, and James T. South, *Disciplinary Practices in Pauline Texts* (Lewistown, NY: Mellen Biblical Press, 1992).

pline," a term I dislike because it suggests that corrective discipline is somehow "negative"). This is a valid question, and I should offer an explanation for my methodology. While there are many aspects of spiritual discipline, I have chosen to focus (in the earlier book as well as in this one) on what I believe is the most neglected aspect: *corrective discipline*. For this reason, I will discuss only those texts in which Jesus and various New Testament writers (most notably, Paul*) instruct the church to act in a specifically corrective or defensive manner in response to deviant behavior and/or teaching by members of the Christian community or by outsiders who threaten the church's welfare.* By taking this approach, I hope to give a comprehensive picture of the corrective disciplinary practices of the early church as well as to offer a model for churches to follow today. For the most part, we already know the importance of prayer, worship, private devotions, and Christian fellowship, and there are numerous studies designed to reinforce these practices, but we know precious little of corrective discipline. My prayer is that this book will help remedy that gap in our thinking and experience.

Likewise, I have again chosen not to discuss the legal issues which sometimes surround the practice of church discipline, although this is a genuine concern of many. However, too often we have put the cart before the horse by worrying over the legal ramifications of discipline rather than seeking to understand and put into practice the Lord's will for His people. This isn't to suggest that serious legal, financial, and other consequences might not result from choosing to follow Scripture, but there have always been serious consequences of taking God at His word. It seems to me it is past time for us to devote ourselves as strenuously to finding out what Scripture says about discipline as we have often been devoted to protecting ourselves from its consequences.[4]

---

[4]Much of the concern for the legal ramifications of discipline in recent decades resulted from the much-publicized case of Marian Guinn *vs.* the Collinsville, Oklahoma,

One criticism of my first book was that it did not provide a specific procedural outline for carrying out discipline, and it is true that it did not. Those seeking a list of "steps" to be followed (other than those outlined in various New Testament texts) will again be disappointed, but for what I believe is a valid reason. I'm persuaded that at least part of our difficulty with discipline has been that we have sought to carry it out according to a predetermined sequence of "steps" rather than by prayerfully searching the Scriptures and being guided by the principles it provides on a case-by-case basis. It was and continues to be my conviction that the Bible offers no such lists, because we are to deal with each situation and each person directly, lovingly, and as circumstances require and not according to any manual or handbook.[5]

As with the first book, I would like to repeat my continuing gratitude to my wife, Linda, Pat Langston, Mural Worthey, Robert Oglesby, Philip Slate, Tom Olbricht, and the late Harvey Porter and his wife Sue for their reading of the first manuscript and their invaluable suggestions and encouragement. Also, I continue to be indebted to Neil Lightfoot, who left us to be with the Lord in the past year, for publishing that book and for constantly urging me to write. Likewise, to Flavil Yeakley, Jr., Jimmy Jividen, and Howard Norton for their contributions and suggestions for the first book. I also hereby express appreciation to all of those who read the original work and for those who reviewed it in print.

Church of Christ. For details of the case, see Flavil R. Yeakley, Jr., "Implications for Church Discipline in the Case of Guinn vs. the Collinsville Church of Christ," a paper presented at the Conference on the Rule of Christ, Goshen College, Goshen, Indiana, 1992. Also, various articles and editorials in *The Christian Chronicle* (April, 1984). For documentation of the effects of the Collinsville case on attitudes toward discipline among Churches of Christ, see Robert E. Whiddon, Jr., "The Current State of the Practice of Church Discipline in the Churches of Christ in America" (Unpublished Ph.D. dissertation, Trinity Theological Seminary, 1996).

[5] Those interested in specific procedures for discipline can find several examples in the online articles mentioned above.

Each of these has provided a special form of fellowship for which I am grateful and which will help make this second book perhaps even more useful than the first.

A special word of thanks is in order to Philip Slate for graciously consenting to write the Foreword to this book. As a firm believer in the necessity and efficacy of church discipline, he has offered me, as well as many others, much encouragement over the years and continues to serve as a marvelous example of one who takes seriously the biblical injunction to love the Lord with all of one's mind.

Richmond, Virginia
August, 2014

ONE

Why All the Neglect?

Discipline is a Thing so little known to us, and that of the Primitive Church has hitherto lain involved in such a Number of voluminous Writers, that the drawing it thence into a clear and open Light would, I conceived, be a Thing of much Use and Benefit. So that if I have performed this Part well and faithfully, I am not without Hope, that I have done a good Work. Whether I have so performed, or not, the Reader must judge for himself upon Tryal made of it. (Nathaniel Marshall, *The Penitential Discipline of the Primitive Church*, 1714)

In a series of classes on church discipline at a university Bible lectureship, I began by taking what is admittedly an unscientific survey but one which is nevertheless revealing. I asked the group of about one hundred ministers, elders, and deacons to raise their hands if they represented churches of fewer than one hundred members. That was more than half the group. Next I asked for a show of hands of those from churches ranging from one hundred to two hundred, then two to five hundred, and finally five hundred and more. Not surprisingly, as church size increased, the representation in the class decreased. In fact, there was only one person present from a church of five hundred or more. I then asked for a show of hands of those who had personally experienced corrective congregational discipline in the churches where they worshiped. Only a few hands went up.

I mention this because I think it shows two things: First, not that many Christians are interested in church discipline, and the larger the church, the less likely its leaders (and, by extension, its members) are to be interested in it. Second, even among those who *are* interested in the subject, not much corrective discipline actually occurs. Everyone who has thought about it is aware of this, but no one seems to know what to do about it, so the general neglect of discipline continues.

As indicated in the subtitle of this book, my view of church discipline is that it is God's gift to the church so that we might have healthier congregations. I'm convinced that God built discipline into the fabric of His church because it will make us stronger when practiced consistently and lovingly. Consider the sheer quantity of teaching on this subject in the New Testament:[1]

Why We Should Discipline...

The root of church discipline goes back to Jesus Himself, who taught in Matthew 18.15–17 that awareness of a sinning brother or sister means we should go to that person privately in hopes of regaining him or her, then as necessary expand the circle of those involved in order to bring about repentance. The fact that our Lord foresaw the necessity of such actions should be sufficient cause to motivate us to practice discipline, but sadly it isn't.

Most of the New Testament instructions regarding congregational discipline come from the apostle Paul. He told the Galatians to "restore" those overtaken in sin with gentleness and humility (Gal 6.1). The Thessalonians needed to "keep away from any brother who is walking in idleness" and to "have nothing to do with" those who refused Paul's instructions (2 Thess 3.6–15).

---

[1] Each of these texts are discussed in detail in later chapters. In those chapters I provide my own translation of the key texts under discussion. Otherwise, biblical quotations are from the English Standard Version.

His most extensive instructions on this subject are (not surprisingly) to the church at Corinth, where a man "living with his father's wife" needed to be "delivered to Satan" (1 Cor 5.1–8) and later needed to be forgiven by the church (2 Cor 2.5–11). It wasn't only immorality, however, that concerned Paul, for he told Titus to warn a "factious" person no more than twice, then have nothing more to do with him (Tit 3.10–11) and warned the church at Rome to "watch out for" and "avoid" those who served their own appetites at the expense of the doctrine they had been taught (Rom 16.17–20). In both of his letters to Timothy, Paul instructed his young protégé to correct those whose teachings were not in accord with the truth as taught by Paul (1 Tim 1.3–4; 2 Tim 2.24–26), a practice which he himself had followed (1 Tim 1.18–20). In a similar manner, John ("the elder") declared his intention to deal with the domineering ways of someone named Diotrephes when he came for a visit (3 John 5–11), and he warned "the elect lady" (obviously a church) not to offer hospitality or even a greeting to those who did not "abide in the teaching of Christ" (2 John 9–10).

Even such a brief overview sufficiently demonstrates that corrective discipline was part of everyday church life during its first century of existence and that it ought to be part of the church's life today. Yet we know it isn't. The question is, why? Why do we ignore these Scriptures and their obvious implications for today's church? Why do we refuse to practice something that obviously has a prominent place in God's plan for the church, even as we claim to utilize the Scriptures as our guide?

…But Why We Don't

Clearly I don't know all the answers to these questions, but allow me to offer some suggestions.

1. *There is an absence of adequate models for us to follow.* The vast majority of today's Christians have absolutely no experience what-

ever with the practice of corrective discipline. Those who do have often seen it practiced poorly and conclude, based on their negative experiences, it can't be done in a constructive way.

Following a Sunday morning service during which our congregation had disciplined someone publicly, my phone rang that afternoon. It was one of our members who had been with us only a year or so and who had been a Christian for only a few years, and he asked a revealing question: "What was that that we did this morning?" It was a sincere question from an honest heart, and after a few minutes' explanation with reference to several of the texts listed above, he understood the rationale for our collective action. He even added that he wished something like that had been done in the church where he previously worshiped because of an adulterous church leader whose example had ruined the church's reputation and made community evangelism virtually impossible. This brother represents the majority of church members, even those who have been Christians for years, who simply have never seen discipline practiced.

On the other hand, when churches have attempted to practice discipline, it has often been carried out so poorly (and destructively) that those who witnessed it hope never to do so again. Consider this typical scenario: The minister of a church begins to notice all the Bible has to say on the subject of church discipline and persuades the church's elders that they should begin to practice it. So they put together a list of "delinquent" members, many of whom haven't attended in years and whom most don't even remember, and notify them by mail that they must repent by a certain date or face congregational discipline. After the deadline passes, further contact is attempted by the church's elders, but in most instances they don't even get to talk to the people they were seeking. Another letter goes out, warning the impenitent that, unless they respond by a certain date, the church will publicly withdraw its fellowship from them. Again, no response. So the threat is carried out by a designated elder who reads the list on the appointed day and expresses the elders' regret that none have repented. At first not much is said, but then the grumbling begins. Someone points out that a friend of one of the elders is conspicuously absent from the list, as are some prominent members of the community who are as delinquent (maybe more so) as those on the list. There are a few heated exchanges in church business meetings; then the whole thing dies down but not without leaving scars that will remain for a lifetime. From that point on when anyone talks about discipline, a wall immediately goes up; corrective discipline is no longer an acceptable topic—let alone practice—in that church for decades to come.

So when people do want to take Scripture seriously and are genuinely concerned about people whose lives have gone astray, they have no adequate models to follow; they simply haven't seen it done or, in some cases, done well.

2. *We suffer from a shortage of genuine fellowship.* As we will see later, discipline properly done is an outgrowth of our fellowship in Christ. When Jesus spoke of going to a sinner, He called him "your brother" and made it clear the goal is the preservation or restoration of fellowship among believers. But in the absence of genuine fellowship, corrective discipline will be ineffective at best and abusive at worst. Discipline can only be effective when people know and care about one another. Too often we know one another only superficially, not sufficiently to try to intervene when they are in spiritual trouble, which is what discipline is about. So a church can't just decide to "start a program of discipline"; rather, it must first focus on intensive fellowship.

3. *There is frequent misunderstanding of the pastoral role of elders.* Hebrews 13.17 makes clear that church leaders "will have to give account" for the souls in their care. Yet how many elders accept their responsibilities with any thought at all that this involves the practice of discipline? Scripture teaches that elders are likewise "shepherds." (See Acts 20.28, where the phrase "care for the church of God" is literally "shepherd the church of God." Likewise see 1 Peter 5.1–2 where Peter instructs the "elders" [v 1] to "shepherd the flock of God that is among you, exercising oversight" [v 2].) Elders, shepherds (pastors), and overseers (bishops) all seem to have been designations for the same role in New Testament times. And what's more inherent in the role of a shepherd than reclaiming lost sheep? Yet somehow we have come to see elders more as decision-makers and less as true pastors of God's people. So when problems arise they are unprepared to take action, and churches generally don't expect them to do so.

As I demonstrate in a later chapter, elders are not solely responsible for the practice of discipline, as indicated by the fact that when Paul speaks of disciplinary action he always speaks to the church as a whole, not just to its leaders. Still, it is unlikely that discipline—especially the public variety—will ever take place unless the elders lead the church to do so. Somebody has to lead the way in shepherding the flock.

4. *We fail to love as God loves.* It is beyond dispute that God disciplines those He loves (Heb 12.4–10; Rev 3.19), yet when someone raises the subject of church discipline, a frequent objection is that it's "unloving" to discipline as Scripture teaches us to do. Aside from the fact that such an opinion places us at odds with what the Bible teaches, there is a logical inconsistency here: it is no more "unloving" for the church to discipline each other than it is for God to discipline us. In fact, as Jonathan Lee-

man argues, "By abstaining from discipline...we claim that we love better than God loves, since God disciplines those He loves.[2] What is truly unloving is to watch people adopt destructive behavior, both to themselves and to the church, and do nothing about it. The opposite of love isn't hatred; it's indifference. This seems to be the point of Leviticus 19.17–18: "You shall not hate your brother in your heart, but you shall reason frankly with your neighbor, lest you incur sin because of him. You shall not take vengeance or bear a grudge against the sons of your own people, but you shall love your neighbor as yourself: I am the Lord." The people of Israel, as part of their commonly-held covenant relationship with God, were to behave in ways that expressed love (i.e., genuine concern) for one another. This included discussing a brother's sins with him face to face when needed. To fail to do so constituted hatred. These verses must surely underlie Jesus' words: "If your brother sins against you, go and tell him his fault, between you and him alone" (Matt 18.15). Surely Jesus did not teach us to do that which is unloving.

When I was very young our neighbor's house caught fire in the middle of the night. We knew these people well, and they were liked and respected in the small town where I grew up. We went to church with them, and one of their sons was a close friend of mine. So when their house caught fire, was it unloving that someone who saw the flames sounded the alarm and woke them up? After all, it was very late and they were sound asleep. To ask such a question is to answer it: the unloving thing to do is nothing. It may be *easier* to do nothing, but it's certainly anything but *loving*.

5. *We're not convinced it will really help.* Where discipline is concerned, we've often replaced faith with fear, the fear that we'll do more harm than good or that our efforts, unpleasant and difficult

---

[2] *Church Discipline: How the Church Protects the Name of Jesus* (Wheaton, IL: Crossway, 2012), 23.

as they are, will simply be wasted. When fear prevails, motivation is absent. What this amounts to is simply a failure to take God at His word. We prefer our own methods of "tolerance" to God's demand for discipline. We need to be rebuked and corrected by Scripture (2 Tim 3.16–17).

6. *We are overly influenced by our permissive culture.* In an excellent article on church discipline, Albert Mohler Jr. says, "Put simply, the abandonment of church discipline is linked to American Christianity's creeping accommodation to American culture." He goes on to point out that, as American culture has adopted the viewpoint of moral individualism (nothing is really "sinful," since there are no absolutes that apply to everyone), churches have for the most part ceased even to speak of discipline, let alone practice it.[3] We may continue to insist that we are "guided by Scripture," but the abandonment of the apostolic practice of church discipline demonstrates that we are influenced even more by the standards of society around us. As has been often observed it isn't a problem for a ship to be on the ocean, since it was built for that. But when the ocean gets into the ship, there is serious danger. How can we deny that we are in fact saturated with our culture's view of morality and discipline rather than that of Scripture?

So far all I've done is identify the problem, a necessary first step to making real changes in our thinking. But identifying the problem isn't the same as rectifying it. Why and how we can accomplish that is the subject of the rest of this book.

---

[3] R. Albert Mohler Jr., "Church Discipline: The Missing Mark," *The Highway*, www.the-highway.com/discipline_Mohler.html (accessed 29 Aug. 2014). This article is also Chapter 8 in *The Compromised Church: The Present Evangelical Crisis*, ed. John H. Armstrong (Wheaton, IL: Crossway Books, 1998).

For Thought and Discussion

1. Do you agree that the size of a church affects whether or not it is likely to engage in corrective discipline? Why or why not? What size church do you attend? Does the church practice discipline?

2. Do you think most Christians are aware of what the New Testament says about discipline? What does this suggest about the effectiveness of the church's adult teaching program? About individual Christians' personal Bible study? About the priorities of most church leaders?

3. Among the reasons discussed in this chapter for the general lack of discipline in most churches, which one would you single out as primary? Can you think of other reasons you would add to this list?

4. Why do people tend to see church discipline as unloving? What does this say about their understanding of love?

5. If you are or have been a member of a church that practiced public corrective discipline, what is your opinion of how it was carried out? In your opinion, was it effective? Why or why not? What could or should have been done differently?

TWO

Discipline as the Pursuit of Holiness

God has graciously joined Himself to His people, the church, which has become the new temple of God. ... As such He comes to the church as the Holy One, demanding the reflection of His character in His temple: "You shall be holy, for I am holy." (Art Arzurdia, "Recovering the Third Mark of the Church," *Reformation & Revival*, Fall, 1994)

I've thought a great deal about why corrective discipline, as evident as it is in the New Testament, has never quite caught hold in the modern church and is even opposed by a significant number of Christians. One reason, I'm persuaded, is our failure to see discipline in its proper theological context. How does discipline fit into the larger framework of biblical revelation? How does it relate to other important biblical themes? Too often we think of discipline as simply arising out of a smattering of isolated, arbitrary commands, and as a result too much of our teaching has been in proof-text fashion, quoting the relevant texts without regard to their immediate contexts or to the wider context of the Bible in general. As a result, we tend to think of discipline as something which we must do simply because it is a Scriptural practice, with little understanding of why Scripture says what it does. As a result, Christians generally remain unconvinced of the importance of discipline. So we should go deeper into the word in order to understand what discipline is and why it is important.

As believers, we should be convinced that God is never arbitrary but that there is always a purpose behind His words. Sometimes He chooses to reveal His reasoning, and sometimes He doesn't. Deuteronomy 29.29 draws a distinction between "the things that have been revealed" and those that have not. So we need to accept the fact that we will never know some of God's reasons for what He says and does. In the case of corrective church discipline, however, we *are* told the reasons behind it, but we've generally overlooked the explanations. Discipline, the writer of Hebrews tells us, arises out of the very nature of God Himself. We must discipline ourselves and one another so that we will become more like our Creator. This aspect of His nature toward which we must be led can be summarized in one word: *holiness*.

Holiness in Hebrews

Holiness isn't exactly one of the hot topics among churches and Christians today. Given the permissive world in which we live, it's a concept that seems out of touch and one not likely to appeal to those we are trying to get inside our doors. All too often we think of holiness primarily in terms of what we should *not* do as part of our isolation from the world and worldly things. Without doubt this is an important aspect of holiness (see Jas 1.27 for example), but it is only one aspect. God has not sent us into the world to be monks cloistered away in the confines of our own inner circles; rather, He has sent us to be lights to the world, beacons to show a better Way (John 14.6). Likewise, even though doing good is part of holiness, holiness is not an achievement which we attain for ourselves by doing good.

To understand holiness properly, we must begin not with ourselves but with God, whose essential nature is holiness. In Isaiah's vision of the Lord, the seraphim called out, "Holy, holy, holy is the Lord of hosts; the whole earth is full of his glory" (Is 6.3). So deeply did this vision of God and His holiness impress Isaiah that he called God "the Holy One of Israel" some 26 times. And God's instruction to Israel was "You shall therefore be holy, for I am holy" (Lev 11.44–45). Israel's character was to arise from and reflect the holy character of her God. Peter echoes this concept in regard to Christians in 1 Peter 1.14–16: "As obedient children, do not be conformed to the passion of your former ignorance, but as he who called you is holy, you also be holy in all your conduct, since it is written, 'You shall be holy, for I am holy.'" Holiness, as applied to God, is His differentness, His "otherness," His uniqueness. Rudolf Otto described Him as "the Wholly Other,"[1] the one who is all that we are not and who exists in utter perfection. To worship such a God is to acknowledge the call to become holy as He is holy.

The Christians to whom Hebrews was originally written were in grave danger of giving up their faith in Christ and reverting to their former Jewish religion. Apparently due to discouragement, persecution, and a failure to grasp the uniqueness of their Savior, they were contemplating trading their new faith for the old. (According to 10.24–25 some had already done so.)[2] One way the author seeks to bolster their shaking faith is to point them to the uniqueness of Jesus and of the salvation He offers. This is where the concept of holiness comes in: what Jesus brought to them came from the all-holy God, and they dare not abandon it or take it lightly (Heb 12.25–29).[3]

---

[1] Rudolf Otto, *The Idea of the Holy*, trans. John W. Harvey (New York: Oxford University Press, 1958), 24ff.

[2] Some scholars question this reconstruction of the situation of Hebrews' first readers, but it still seems to me that it best fits the evidence of the letter itself.

[3] The adjective *hagios* ("holy") and related terms occur twenty-six times in Hebrews. It is derived from the old Greek term *hagos* which denotes an object of awe. The adjec-

Stephen Neill aptly describes Hebrews as "a letter which contains in germ everything that needs to be said about [holiness]."[4] The author of Hebrews calls his readers "holy brothers" (3.1) and "saints" ("holy ones"—6.10; 13.24), and he stresses that they have been "sanctified" ("made holy") by the blood of Christ (2.11; 9.13; 10.10, 14; 13.12) and warns them that turning away from Christ means profaning the blood of the covenant by which they had been sanctified (10.29). There is frequent reference in Hebrews to the "Holy" Spirit (2.4; 3.7; 9.8; 10.15), and Jesus ministers in the true "sanctuary" ("holy place") versus the old earthly one (8.2; 9.1–3, 12, 24–25; 10.19; 13.11). Jesus is our high priest, "holy (*hosios*),[5] innocent, unstained, separated from sinners, and exalted above the heavens." "So Jesus also suffered outside the gate in order to sanctify the people through his own blood. Therefore let us go to him outside the camp and bear the reproach he endured" (13.12–13).

But Hebrews goes even further. We are not only called to be holy; our holiness is absolutely imperative: "Strive for peace with everyone, *and for the holiness without which no one will see the Lord*" (12.14). The failure to attain holiness is to "fail to obtain the grace of God," to become "defiled," "immoral," and "unholy" (12.15–16).

---

tive *hages* means "clean," and the verb *hazo* suggests shrinking back from something. *Hagios* is used to describe sanctuaries ("holy places") and is later applied to gods and religious practices. In the New Testament holiness expresses God's innermost nature and embraces the concepts of omnipotence, eternity, and glory which evoke awe. See D. Proksch and O. Proksch, "*hagios*, etc." in *Theological Dictionary of the New Testament*, ed. G. Kittel and G. Friedrich; abridged in one volume by G.W. Bromiley (Grand Rapids: Eerdmans, 1985) 14–16.

[4] *Christian Holiness* (London: Lutterworth, 1960) 110.

[5] In Classical Greek *hosios* denotes what is in accordance with divine direction and providence or is sanctioned or hallowed by divine or natural law. "The use of *hosios* in Heb. 7.26 is unique. Here the word is used absolutely in the way in which elsewhere it can be used only of God. As high priest Christ is *hosios*, utterly without sin and utterly pure, so that his offering is sufficient once and for all" (H. Seebass, *The New International Dictionary of New Testament Theology*, Vol. 2, ed. Colin Brown [Grand Rapids: Zondervan, 1976] 236–38).

For you have not come to what may be touched, a blazing fire and darkness and gloom and a tempest and the sound of a trumpet and a voice whose words made the hearers beg that no further messages be spoken to them. ... But you have come to Mount Zion and to the city of the living God, the heavenly Jerusalem, and to innumerable angels in festal gathering, and to the assembly of the firstborn who are enrolled in heaven, and to God, the judge of all, and to the spirits of the righteous made perfect, and to Jesus, the mediator of a new covenant, and to the sprinkled blood that speaks a better word than the blood of Abel. See that you do not refuse him who is speaking (12.18–25).

Obviously this business of holiness is of vastly greater importance than we have often realized.

Yet it is exactly here that we come face to face with a problem: How can we, who are sinful, ever be holy? The solution begins with the realization that Jesus, our High Priest, is holy (7.26). And, as Hebrews explains, by the shedding of His blood, we are *made holy*, much as the sprinkling with blood made holy the vessels in the temple (9.13; 10.10, 14; 13.12). So holiness (sanctification) is, in one sense, a gift which God gives us when we turn to Christ and are baptized into Him (Acts 2.38; 22.16; 1 Cor 6.11; etc.).

Still, Hebrews calls on us to *be* holy and to *strive for holiness*, indicating that our sanctification is in some way incomplete even after conversion. But this thought isn't unique to Hebrews. In several of his letters Paul follows the pattern known as the indicative followed by the imperative, in which he states who and what we *are* as a result of being in Christ, then tells us what we must *do* in order to act out what we are and become even more so. For example, in Ephesians 1–3, Paul says we are in Christ, saved by grace, and now constitute the "new humanity" created by the cross. Then in 4.1 he says, "I therefore, a prisoner for the Lord, urge you to walk in a manner worthy of the calling to which you have been called," and specifically outlines in the remainder of the letter what that "worthy manner" entails. So we *are* holy through the blood of Christ, but we must *pursue* that holiness and develop and maintain it each day of our lives.[6] And the "indicative" aspect of our faith—who we are because of what Christ has done for us on the cross—provides us with sufficient motivation to become all that God has called us to be: His holy people.

Holiness and Discipline

Hebrews 12.7–11 makes the explicit connection between holiness and discipline:

> It is for discipline that you have to endure. God is treating you as sons. For what son is there whom His father does not discipline? If you are left without discipline, then you are illegitimate children and not sons. Besides this, we have had earthly fathers who disciplined us and we respected them. Shall we not much more be subject to the Father of spirits and live? For they disciplined us for a short time as it seemed best to them, but he disciplines us for our good, *that we may share his holiness.* For the moment all discipline seems painful rather than pleasant, but later it yields the peaceful fruit of righteousness to those who have been trained by it.

Holiness doesn't come easily for any of us. Since our sinful nature is so far from God's all-holy nature, we require considerable

---

[6] "Holiness is a state into which we have been brought by the offering of the body of Jesus once for all; but it is realized only in a constantly renewed obedience to the One who was himself obedient… Christian holiness, whether for the Church or for the individual, can never be a static thing, something gained once for all. It has to be maintained amid conflicts and perils that are renewed day by day. It is a moving thing; it can only exist as a function of pilgrimage" (Neill, 111–12).

refinement. In ways we may not even realize, we lack the holiness which God requires, and this is where discipline comes in.

In Hebrews 12.7–11 the writer addresses his readers' situation of experiencing persecution. Perhaps to their surprise, he describes this reality not as an unfortunate circumstance by which they were being victimized, but as "the discipline of the Lord." There's no indication in this paragraph that God was in some way punishing these Christians or that He was angry with them.[7] Rather, "God is treating you as sons" (v 7b). In comparing the discipline we receive from our earthly fathers to that of our heavenly Father, the author points out that the former disciplined us temporarily "as it seemed best to them," even though their discipline may have been inappropriate. Human parents naturally make many mistakes in disciplining their children. But God "disciplines us for our good, that we may share his holiness" (v 10).[8] According to Hebrews, God's discipline "trains" us so that it yields in us "the peaceful fruit of righteousness" (v 11). As he continues, the writer admonishes his readers to accept this discipline and to "Strive... for holiness" (vv 12–15). God doesn't wish simply to forgive us; He also wants us to share His essential nature and to become like Himself. "The end result in salvation is not that we should be left much as we were at the beginning but that we should be remade

---

[7] The presence of the terms "reproves" ("punishes" in RSV) and "chastises" in verses 5–6 does not necessarily indicate that the readers of Hebrews were being punished. Rather, these terms are part of the quotation from Proverbs 3.11–12, which the author cites because it teaches the principle that God disciplines those He loves (even if they are or are not being punished by Him).

[8] "Earthly discipline confines itself to the sphere of earthly life; but heavenly discipline, which is never arbitrary, seeks to purge God's own from sin and secure for them a permanent participation in the divine life, whose essential requirement is holiness." (Neil R. Lightfoot, *Jesus Christ Today: A Commentary on the Book of Hebrews* [Grand Rapids: Baker, 1976], 223. Reprinted and now available in paperback from Bible Guides, 16415 Addison Rd., Suite 800, Addison, TX 75001).

in the likeness of God."[9] This is what discipline is all about. But we must accept God's discipline and trust that He has a benevolent purpose, one which is entirely in our best interest.[10]

All spiritual discipline, therefore, is the outgrowth of God's desire for us to share His holiness. This includes not only the discipline that sometimes comes from persecution or opposition, but also disciplining ourselves and one another. This is where "striving after holiness" comes in: We must decide that we want God's holiness and are willing to pursue it according to the teachings of His word. This means disciplining ourselves to worship, pray, serve, study, and live out God's word in our lives while resisting the tendencies of the flesh which war against those of the Holy Spirit (Gal 5.17). If we fail to accept this aspect of God's discipline, we will not be holy, and ultimately we will not "see the Lord."

In the same manner congregational discipline is an extension of God's desire for our holiness. Just as God expects and requires us to discipline ourselves, He calls on us to discipline each other when necessary, not in an arbitrary or angry or vengeful way but as an outgrowth of His love and of His demand for holiness among His people. *It is no more "unloving" for us to discipline one another in the interest of holiness than it is for God to discipline us for the same purpose.* In fact, as Hebrews asserts, the lack of discipline is a distinctly un-God-like characteristic.

"But," someone might object, "Hebrews doesn't talk about *church* discipline, so is it legitimate to connect what it says about God's discipline to corrective congregational discipline?" The an-

---

[9] Leon Morris, *Bible Study Commentary: Hebrews* (Grand Rapids: Zondervan, 1983), 123.

[10] "The clear implication of verse 10 is that it is impossible to share in God's holiness apart from the correction administered through disciplinary sufferings, which have the effect of maturing us as men and women of God" (William L. Lane, *Call to Commitment* [Nashville: Thomas Nelson, 1985], 164).

swer is yes. Although Hebrews never explicitly discusses such actions as the withdrawal of fellowship or avoiding another believer in order to bring him to repentance, it certainly implies congregational discipline. For example, Hebrews 12.15–16 continues the discussion of discipline by saying, "See to it that no one fails to obtain the grace of God; that no 'root of bitterness' springs up and causes trouble, and by it many become defiled; that no one is sexually immoral or unholy like Esau, who sold his birthright for a single meal." Clearly, the body as a whole is charged with the responsibility to exert some measure of control on one another's behavior, not only to avoid a few being lost but to prevent "many" from becoming defiled. Similar exhortations occur in 3.12–14 and 4.11, and 10.24–25 strikes an obvious note of communal responsibility when it says, "And let us consider how to stir up one another to love and good works, not neglecting to meet together as is the habit of some, but encouraging one another, and all the more as you see the Day drawing near."

And it isn't only Hebrews which makes the holiness/discipline connection. In the notorious case of incest which was uncorrected at Corinth, Paul warned the church that "a little leaven leavens the whole lump" (1 Cor 5.6). Borrowing from Israel's Passover/Exodus experience, he warned the church that their holiness was threatened by the presence of undisciplined sin in their midst. And just as Israel had to remove the old leaven, so Paul admonished the Corinthians to "Purge the evil person from among you" (v 13). The "purge out" formula occurs frequently in Deuteronomy following specific commands to the Israelites which were important for maintaining their holiness as the people of God. Likewise in Matthew 18.17 Jesus commands that the "brother who sins" and cannot be persuaded to repent should "be to you as a Gentile and a tax collector." Both categories of individuals were considered to have a defiling influence on righteous Jews and were thus to be avoided (Ex 23.23–33, etc.). So Jesus teaches that His holy followers must avoid unrepentant offenders in the interest of preserving their holiness. It is impossible to maintain holiness in the absence of discipline, both of ourselves and of others who insist on living unholy lives.[11]

Holiness and Survival

For a variety of reasons (some of which I have already discussed) we have drifted far in today's church from the biblical concept of holiness preserved by discipline. In reality, we don't speak nearly as much about the need for holiness as did our spiritual ancestors, and many seem to believe that we can maintain holiness apart from discipline.

One concern often expressed is that discipline will cause problems that will hinder the church's growth by turning off those we are trying to reach with the gospel. The mere fact that we believe obeying a biblical practice will hinder the church from becoming what God desires it to be indicates how shallow our understanding of holiness is. What about the negative influence of un-repented sin in our midst, a reality which shouts to the unbelieving world that we aren't nearly as serious about sin and redemption as we claim?

John White and Ken Blue, in their stimulating book on church discipline, make the following observation:

Why is it that the thought of a holy and godly church concerns us so little? While the church of past centuries focused too much on

---

[11] If the objection is raised that Jesus "defiled" Himself by associating with tax collectors, sinners, and, occasionally, Gentiles, it should be noted that these were not yet part of His following but were people showing signs of repentance leading to inclusion in the kingdom. They were not unrepentant believers whose lives had taken a turn away from kingdom principles.

purity to the exclusion of the other goals of corrective discipline, we have ignored it entirely too much. As stated earlier, we have become calloused to sin. To our great shame, *holiness* has become an empty word. Can it be because we have other goals for the church which supersede her holiness? Does our preoccupation with building programs, with our public image in the community, with our innovative programming or with our church growth suffocate our concern for the holiness of God's people?

We are blind. As churches we no longer see God. Only the pure in heart see him and our hearts are no longer pure. We even forget that we are at war. The hosts of wickedness are doing all they can to befoul the bride of Jesus. How better could they express their hatred of him? If you are honest you will admit that at times it is hard to conceive the ferocity and the intensity of the battles in heavenly places, the heinous and implacable will of evil to destroy and to mar anything that bears the name of Jesus. And so we play church while the fires of hell rage round us. What ought we to be doing? We ought to be exercising corrective church discipline. It is a matter of life and death for the church.[12]

In the years since White and Blue wrote these penetrating words, think of all that has happened in the world morally and spiritually. Christians only a generation ago could hardly have imagined that their descendants today would be living in a society where same-sex marriage would be legalized and where people would be so self-focused that even some Christians believe that virtually anything they want to do should be either ignored or approved by the church. In such an era of incredibly lax standards, there is a powerful temptation for the church to neglect discipline in the interest of maintaining relevance to the world around us. After all, won't we seem more than a little out

---

[12] John White and Ken Blue, *Healing the Wounded: The Costly Love of Church Discipline* (Downers Grove, IL: InterVarsity, 1985), 59.

of touch if we insist on holiness while others insist there are no moral absolutes at all? Aren't we only hurting ourselves and the cause of Christ by doing something that seems so bizarre and outdated? In an era when being "judgmental" is about the worst thing one can do, doesn't practicing church discipline cause us to cut our own throats?

We fail to see is that it is precisely *because* of these attitudes that discipline is perhaps more necessary than ever. The secular influences of immorality, materialism, and self-centeredness threaten to engulf the church to an unprecedented degree. It may have been the case that in the predominantly "Christian society" in which many of us grew up, the church could refrain from discipline without much immediate effect. After all, our standards were, in many places at least, basically the same as most of society around us. But we no longer have the luxury (if indeed we ever had it) of allowing sin to go uncorrected in our midst. Now discipline is a matter of survival. If we don't resist the ungodly influences of the world through discipline, the world will transform us into its own image rather than our being transformed into the likeness of Christ.

God disciplines us "that we may share his holiness," and without His holiness "no one will see the Lord." Dare we refuse to discipline? Dare we allow ourselves to remain comfortable in our disobedience?

For Thought and Discussion

1. If someone were to ask, "Are you holy?" how would you likely respond? Why? What would your answer say about your understanding of holiness?

2. What images does the word "holiness" bring to your mind? Positive images? Negative?

3. In what sense is holiness something which we already have and yet something toward which we must strive? Give some concrete examples of both kinds of holiness.

4. What kinds of discussions (sermons, Bible classes, etc.) about holiness have you heard in the church? Were they helpful or not? Why?

5. Explain in your own words the connection between discipline and sharing the holiness of God. Why is discipline a necessary corollary to our holiness?

THREE

No Discipline, No Church[1]

Even if it may not be this week's fad in American theology, something of the nature of church discipline has always been part of the life of the people of God. (Marlin Jeschke, *Discipling in the Church*)

Everyone at the West Side church was shocked at the unbelievable news that one of their most beloved and active members had left his wife of more than twenty years for another woman. Ron had been a Bible class teacher, an effective personal evangelist, a fellowship group leader, as well as a seemingly model husband and father. His adultery had a strangely numbing effect on the congregation. No one even wanted to talk about what had happened, and nothing was ever said—at least not openly—about disciplining him. Ron was just there one day and gone the next. But in spite of his sin, Ron's faith meant too much to him to be forgotten, and he missed his active role in the church. So a few years later he re-surfaced at a congregation across town, bringing his new wife with him and asking to be accepted as a member but with no indication of repentance.

Meanwhile, members from West Side occasionally encoun-

---

[1] The title of this chapter is borrowed from the title of an article by Kenneth R. Davis, "No Discipline, No Church: An Anabaptist Contribution to the Reformed Tradition," *Sixteenth Century Journal* XIII No. 4 (1982), 43–58.

tered Ron socially. At first it was really awkward for them to be around him, but Ron didn't act as if anything were wrong, and soon the discomfort left for most people, although several had serious questions about how they should regard him or if they should associate with him at all. After all, he had committed adultery and hadn't repented of it. But then, he hadn't been disciplined, so no one knew exactly what to do. The situation didn't change much until several years later when Ron became seriously ill and died, with nothing having been done to try to bring him to repentance.

Keeping the Fences in Good Repair

Ron's fictionalized but oft-repeated story raises some difficult dilemmas. Exactly what was Ron's standing with the church? Since he was never formally disciplined at West Side or made any move to withdraw his membership there, was he still a member? And, since he wasn't disciplined where he had first been a member, what should the leadership of the second congregation have done about him, assuming they had known about his adultery? Could he have become a member there, or should he have returned to West Side and "made things right" there? If the second congregation had refused to grant him membership, on what grounds would they have done so? What if he had left that church, moved away, and become identified with a third church that knew nothing of him or his past? And what is the spiritual status of a church that becomes filled with "Rons"? Does God still recognize it as His church? If not, at what point does it cease to be so? And what of Ron's friends at his old congregation? Should they have continued to be friendly and socialize with him as if nothing had ever happened in hopes he would someday come to his senses? Or should they have exercised a personal responsibility to avoid him, even though the church as a whole had not responded to his sin?

At this point we're talking about a function of church disci-pline known among social scientists as "boundary maintenance." Any group, religious or otherwise, which claims unique status must have and maintain clearly-demarcated boundaries so all can recognize who is and who is not in the group. Otherwise, group membership loses all meaning. And if boundaries are to be maintained, there must be some process by which members who violate the norms of the group (i.e., put themselves outside the group boundaries) can be identified and/or sanctioned or even removed. The church of Christ is no exception to this. In fact, it is uniquely true of the church, since we claim, based on the teach-ings of Scripture, to be the people of God and since the Bible gives us the guidelines by which God's people are called to live. We must recognize the inescapable conclusion that discipline is a necessary corollary to the nature of the church as it is described in the Bible. In other words, "No discipline, no church." Not that this loss of identity happens at a given moment in time or that it can be discerned by the human eye. But the second and third chapters of Revelation state that at some point Christ will "re-move the lampstand" from those churches which violate His will and refuse to repent—and they may not even realize that it has happened.[2] Such loss of spiritual standing with the Lord doesn't happen because we fail to maintain discipline as an "identifying mark of the church" and thereby disqualify ourselves as a New Testament church.[3] If this were true, there would likely be a lot fewer "true churches" than most of us think! Rather churches lose their status with the Lord because the lack of discipline violates

---

[2] In Rev 2.5 the Lord threatens to come and "remove the lampstand" of the church at Ephesus unless they repent of their sins, and 1.20 says "the seven lampstands are the seven churches." So it follows that for a church to have its lampstand removed is to "lose its churchness," that is, its right to be called Christ's church.

[3] This was the understanding of the Protestant Reformers and continues to be the understanding of many others today.

the very nature of the church itself so that being "in" it or "out of" it loses all meaning. K. Brynhof Lyon describes this process as he observed it among his own denomination:

> Through a systematic misunderstanding of our history, Disciples' congregations have often seemed to many persons to be fertile soil for individualistic (really subjectivistic) understandings of the Christian life. At this extreme, this suggests that discipline in almost any sense is nonsense since church members can believe anything they want to believe about what constitutes a fitting enactment of the Christian witness. Yet, clearly, when this becomes the church's "norm" of congregational life, it tends to suggest that the church stands for nothing precisely because it stands for anything.[4]

If we hope to restore the God-intended role of discipline in the church today, we must reclaim the New Testament understanding of the nature of the church. Once we have done that, it should be obvious to any thinking observer that discipline must follow in order to maintain the identity which Scripture says we have as followers of Jesus Christ.

The One and Only Body of Christ

According to the New Testament the early Christians accepted the convictions of Judaism that "God is one" and added that there is "one Lord, Jesus Christ" (1 Cor 8.6). As a corollary to this Paul emphasizes that there is but "one body, the church" (Eph 1.22–23; 4.4–6; 1 Cor 12.12–13). All those outside the

---

[4]"The Discipline of Congregational Life: Prospects and Resources for Renewal," *Midstream* Vol. 26 (July, 1987), 403. Lyon proposes a renewal of congregational discipline as a necessary corrective to this situation. In this same issue, see C. Leonard Allen, "Congregational Life and Discipline: An Historical Perspective," 379–90, who discusses the historical tension between the church and the world and the role of discipline in maintaining the distinction between the two.

body "do not know God" (1 Thess 4.5; Gal 4.8–9). The social expression of this monotheistic conviction is the exclusive unity of the worshipers, which accounts for what one writer calls "the language of belonging" and "the language of separation" which we find so frequently in Paul's letters.[5] The "language of belonging" includes references to church members as "saints" (holy ones, set apart ones—1 Cor 1.2; 2 Cor 1.1; Phil 1.1) and the "elect" (1 Thess 1.4; Rom 8.33; 1 Cor 1.27). In the "language of separation" non-members are "the outsiders" (1 Cor 5.12–13; 1 Thess 4.12), "non-believers," "the unrighteous," and "those who have no standing in the church" (1 Cor 6.1, 4, 9), as well as "those who do not know God" (1 Thess 4.5; Gal 4.8).[6]

With this understanding of the nature of the church in mind, the necessity for discipline becomes evident. The boundary between the church and the world must be maintained, and discipline is one of the God-ordained ways of doing so.

Baptism and the Lord's Supper have special roles in reinforcing the concept of boundary establishment and maintenance. Baptism is the "rite of initiation" by which one becomes part of the church, so that it is relatively clear who is "in" and who is "out" (Rom 6.3–5; 1 Cor 1.16–17; 12.13; Gal 3.26–27). Sociologically speaking, being put out of the church's fellowship might be viewed as the reverse of baptism, although there is no suggestion in Scripture that people who repent and are restored to the church's fellowship must

[5] Wayne Meeks, *The First Urban Christians: The Social World of the Apostle Paul* (New Haven: Yale University Press, 1983), 85 and 94.

[6] "Repetitive use of such special terms for the group and its members plays a role in the process of re-socialization by which an individual's identity is revised and knit together with the identity of the group, especially when it is accompanied by special terms also for 'the outsiders,' 'the world.' By this kind of talk members are taught to conceive of only two classes of humanity: the sect and outsiders" (Meeks, 86). Note that "sect" is Meeks' term for any group which sees itself as distinct from all others and is not a pejorative term.

be re-baptized.[7] Similarly, the Lord's Supper is an act of solidarity for the church, as are more common "fellowship meals." Being barred from participation in these, especially from the Lord's Supper, takes on deep significance, and it isn't surprising that we find references to such disciplinary actions in Paul's letters. For example, Paul says we are "not even to eat" with "anyone who bears the name of brother if he is guilty of sexual immorality or greed, or is an idolater, reviler, drunkard, or swindler" (1 Cor 5.11). Why does Paul focus on *not eating* with such people? Because in the ancient world, as in many cultures today, eating with someone was a sign of acceptance. There is some discussion among scholars as to whether the prohibition against eating with an offending brother or sister means ordinary meals in general or the Lord's Supper in particular, but it seems logical to think Paul meant both. How could one act of refusal have any disciplinary effect without the other? Besides, while the offender may make the decision whether or not to assemble with the church for communion, it is *our* decision whether to meet him for lunch. How can we do either with someone who has flouted the norms of the Christian life and refuses to repent without reinforcing such conduct and compromising the church's solidarity? To do so is to reduce the church's disciplinary act to an ecclesiastical formality that does not influence believers' relationships with one another outside the worship assembly. Paul reminds the Thessalonian church of a rule which he had left them when they were first evangelized: "If anyone is not willing to work, let him not eat" (2 Thess 3.10). This is probably a reference to the church's sharing its common store of food (the "pantry") or to the

---

[7] It is going further than the evidence allows to conclude, as does Leeman (*Church Discipline*, 60), that when a person is put out of the church's fellowship ("excommunicated" is his word), it means he is no longer a Christian. More precisely, it means we are dealing with a Christian who is no longer behaving as one and is therefore deprived of the support and friendship of the group. Declaring him no longer a Christian is for God alone. The church's action merely reflects what the church can observe.

"love feasts" which were part of early Christian assemblies (1 Cor 11.17–22; Jude 12). In both 1 Corinthians and 2 Thessalonians, Paul makes it clear that sharing food is a sign of acceptance and being banned from such meals is an overt act of discipline.

The Church as Family

Closely tied to the concept of the church as the exclusive body of Christ is the concept of the church as a family. This arises from the biblical conception of God as "Father" and believers as His children. Also, since early churches usually met in members' homes, the family became a quite natural model for the Christian community, and this is reinforced by the language of family found in Paul's letters.[8] Such a concept of family unity and loyalty implies the need for discipline. Just as we can see the quite visible effects of a lack of parental discipline within a family, we can see it in many churches, if we will only open our eyes and acknowledge the real problem. Just as we often speak of "dysfunctional" families, there are many dysfunctional churches, and much of the dysfunction is traceable to allowing members to "act out" in negative ways without any consequences.

What the Bible says about warning, admonishing, and avoiding members who sin consistently and excluding them from fellowship when necessary is understandable only in the context of a high degree of cohesion within the body. Where such unity and family identity exists, being disciplined by the group has serious implications for one's sense of belonging and social stability.

The Church as Recipients of Eternal Life

The heart of our faith is, of course, the conviction that Jesus was crucified for our sins and rose from the dead. This leads to the con-

---

[8] For example, "brother" in Rom 8.29; 16.33; 1 Cor 1.1; 5.11; 16.12; 2 Cor 1.1; Phil 2.25; "sister" in Rom 16.1; 1 Cor 7.15; 9.5; Philem 2.

viction that those who follow Christ can also expect to be raised from the dead (1 Cor 15; 1 Thess 4.13–18). Conversely, those outside the body are destined for condemnation (Rom 2.6–8; 8.6–7; 1 Cor 6.9–11; 15.12–19; Gal 6.7–10). Discipline follows inevitably from such a concept. Those within the church must be influenced not to abandon their hope, and the boundary between those headed for salvation and those destined for destruction must be kept sharply distinct (at least to the extent that we can make such distinctions). This task may seem intimidating, but we should remember Jesus' declaration that false prophets are readily recognizable by their fruits (Matt 7.15–20) and Paul's statement that "the works of the flesh are evident" (Gal 5.19). The task of maintaining discipline in the church may be challenging, but it is by no means impossible, and we should be careful not to make excuses for our lack of action by distorting the realities of the situation. Since eternity hangs in the balance, there is simply too much at stake.

Blurred Boundaries

Without consistent, lovingly-applied congregational discipline, it becomes impossible to maintain the boundaries between the church and the world. Members such as Ron come and go—undisciplined, unredeemed, and unreclaimed for Christ. Confusion reigns, as suggested in Ron's story. The church preaches one thing about sin but never backs it up when even its most basic teachings are ignored. People begin to wonder if there really is any difference between "us" and "them" or if this is only a pious figment of our imaginations, a relic of the past that no longer has relevance.

Can we truly call people out of the world through the gospel when the world is so much with us? Can we legitimately claim to be the Lord's people when we steadfastly refuse to discipline ourselves and each other as His word so clearly says we should?

And—at what point does Christ remove the lampstand?

For Thought and Discussion

1. Has there ever been someone like Ron in the congregation where you worship? How was the situation handled? What difficulties did it create?

2. Explain the relationship between baptism and the Lord's Supper and "boundary maintenance" within the church.

3. Does the church today make much use of "insider"/"outsider" language? Why or why not? What are some examples of this type of language that we still use?

4. What is the effect on congregations when the boundaries between who is "in" and who isn't become blurred? How can this be changed?

5. What impact does the blurring of boundaries have on the world's attitude toward the church? The church's attitude toward itself?

FOUR

The Ultimate Expression of Fellowship

"The more bitter the truth, the better the friend who tells it." (Sir Pellinore to King Arthur, Camelot)

Dr. Flavil Yeakley, Jr., tells of a meeting between the elders and deacons of a church at which the elders announced their intention to "withdraw fellowship"[1] from several families who had not attended worship in months, some even in years. Following their announcement one of the deacons asked, "What will they miss once fellowship is withdrawn?" The elders at first didn't understand the question, but the deacon went on to explain that a withdrawal of fellowship could have little meaning or effect if there were no real fellowship to withdraw. It seems that, if fellowship is withdrawn, those being disciplined ought to find themselves *missing* something, shouldn't they? The elders met to consider this point and what they were about to do and at a later meet-

---

[1] Although not a biblical term, "withdraw fellowship" is a term often used for excluding someone from the fellowship of a congregation. Catholics and some others employ the term "excommunication," which means essentially the same thing, although in traditional Catholic teaching it has further-reaching consequences than simply a congregational action and so is perhaps best avoided. The New Testament terminology varies considerably by using general terms of avoidance. (See the appropriate later chapters on the various New Testament disciplinary texts.) Although the practice itself is thoroughly biblical, there is no technical term used consistently in the New Testament to describe it.

ing with the deacons, announced that they were about to begin an effort toward intensive *fellowship* with the same people they had been about to discipline. For several weeks the elders visited these people in their homes, invited them to their own homes for meals, and generally spent time getting acquainted with them and discussing their spiritual needs. In a few months' time most of these people acknowledged their negligence and recommitted themselves to the Lord.[2]

This true story highlights two of the most overlooked aspects of corrective church discipline: (1) It is utterly without meaning outside the context of genuine congregational fellowship, and (2) the exercise of discipline is, in fact, the ultimate expression of fellowship. It is the most we can do to maintain or restore fellowship with a brother or sister who has been overtaken by sin.

Fellowship Before Discipline

In the past some churches, realizing their negligence in the area of discipline, have resolved to rectify the situation by doing exactly what the elders described above were about to do: withdraw their fellowship from people with whom they have had little or no contact. Often those so "disciplined" are people no one in the church really even knows. Any time a church has to search for its members in order to "discipline" them, something is seriously wrong, not only with the church leaders' concept of discipline but with that church's fellowship as well. Outside the context of genuine fellowship, discipline can only be destructive, which is one reason so many have had negative experiences with it. Certainly this isn't the intent of discipline according to Scripture.

In Matthew 18 Jesus instructs His disciples to carry out disciplinary measures in order to "gain your brother." Galatians 6.1 teaches "you who are spiritual" to "restore" anyone overtaken

---

[2] From a personal conversation with Dr. Yeakley, used here with his permission.

in sin, not simply to pronounce sentence and get rid of him. "Brother" is a fellowship word, and it is almost always used in the New Testament when discipline is the topic under discussion.[3] A notable exception to this rule occurs in texts which deal with those whose divisiveness and/or heresy is so severe that they are simply to be avoided (as in Rom 16.17 and Tit 3.10–11; contrast 2 Thess 3.6, 14–15). But other than in these situations, the assumption is always that "the offender" is someone in our midst, someone we know and care about—not just a name on a list from years gone by.[4]

Many have observed that oftentimes cases of congregational discipline are meaningless and ineffective because, as indicated above, there is nothing to withdraw (that is, any real fellowship to be missed). The situation is, I'm afraid, actually much worse than that. Apart from fellowship discipline is not only meaningless, it is abusive. To discipline someone with whom we have not enjoyed real fellowship is much like disciplining a stranger's child: the child may genuinely need discipline, but it isn't our place to administer it. Were we to do so, the discipline could only be traumatic and inexplicable to the child. It's no wonder that so many cases of withdrawing fellowship turn out to be entirely ineffective and leave a bad taste in the mouths of the entire congregation. Where there is no fellowship, there is no valid context for carrying out discipline. One of the first lessons to learn about discipline is that you can't discipline someone you don't really care about. The sad truth is that many congregations

---

[3] The New Revised Standard Version obscures this point in the interest of inclusive language by translating *adelphos* with such terms as "another member of the church," "the member," "that one," and "the offender" in Matthew 18.15–17. Likewise, "my friends" replaces "brothers" in Galatians 6.1.

[4] On the relationship between fellowship and discipline, see Jimmy Jividen, *Koinonia: A Place of Tough and Tender Love* (Nashville: Gospel Advocate, 1989), Section 4, 145–94.

cannot effectively discipline one another because there doesn't exist a sufficient level of fellowship to make such actions meaningful.

> Christian fellowship is to restore what human society has lost through sin. But has it done so? Warmer, deeper fellowships exist among Christians. But they are not common. Who feels safe enough in the average church to open up to fellow Christians, to share the painful, shameful and even the trivial everyday things that community was meant to be all about? How would our confidences be received? With polite boredom? Dismay? Gossip? Instead we hide behind our social masks, enjoying what we can, but never being off our guard. A sociologist studying the average Christian church would see no essential difference in the quality of its human relationships and those of some local club, say a community service group or a country club.[5]

Another Way to Say "I Love You"

Not only is fellowship the appropriate and necessary context for discipline, disciplinary acts are themselves an expression of our fellowship. We discipline *because* we are in fellowship with one another, not because we no longer desire to be. If our fellowship is real and there is genuine love for one another, we cannot simply sit by and watch a brother or sister become entangled in sin and do nothing to reclaim them. What kind of fellowship exists when we see the devastating effects of sin in the life of a fellow Christian yet refuse to express our concern in an open and loving way? Even the most extreme form of discipline, the withdrawal of fellowship, is an expression of fellowship; in fact, it is the ultimate expression of fellowship. It says to the persons disciplined that they are simply too important for us to lose them to Satan

---

[5] White and Blue, 55.

without doing everything within our power to reclaim them, and we would rather be deprived of our association with them for a time now than to be apart from them for all eternity. It's not by accident that Jesus' disciplinary instructions in Matthew 18 come in context immediately after the paragraph about the lost sheep (see chs 6 and 7). It isn't God's will for any of His people to perish, so every brother or sister who strays is to be reclaimed at all cost—even the cost of association with those we love most dearly.[6]

When genuine fellowship exists, we will more readily go to our brothers and sisters as Jesus taught us to do in a spirit of loving concern. The need for withdrawal of fellowship will be rare, because most problems will be resolved before getting to that point. I realize that in the minds of many, the idea of practicing discipline conjures up images of a church where people are frequently and harshly disciplined and where a climate of fear and rigidity prevails. But this will not be the case where fellowship is strong and people care about one another. Brotherly love and corrective discipline are in no way mutually exclusive. On the other hand, where no real fellowship exists, there will be no discipline at all—which is not biblically acceptable—or else only formal disciplinary acts—which will be consistently ineffective.

Communally speaking, fellowship is the reason for discipline to occur and is what gives discipline its impact. The dread of a disruption in fellowship with those we love and with whom we have served and worshiped is a powerful motivator toward conforming to group (i.e., biblical) norms. It isn't easy to bring this kind of pressure on a loved one, but there are times when genuine love requires it. It seems strange that we recognize the necessity

---

[6] Lest we think the joy of fellowship and the sorrow of discipline are somehow incompatible, Paul reminds us that in the context of genuine fellowship we should "Rejoice with those who rejoice" and "weep with those who weep" (Rom 12.15). Such weeping may well come in the context of corrective discipline.

of "tough love" when dealing in secular settings with destructive behavior such as alcohol and drug abuse but conclude that the same approach will be destructive rather than constructive when dealing with sin in the church.

A common objection to the practice of discipline is that it will only embitter those who are disciplined and, as a result, make matters worse. Naturally there are no guarantees that disciplinary measures will be effective in bringing back the sinner, but if our fellowship is real we have to try, assuming we are convinced that those who go away into sin and away from Christ have lost their fellowship with the Lord.

> While it is true that offenders ejected from the local congregation may become embittered and plunge further into sin, it is also true that others discover the disenchantment and miseries of sin. These in turn can awaken a hunger for true spiritual consolation and fellowship, especially if the offender left a church flaming with true koinonia, warmed by a faithful, loving Christian fellowship. Cold is never so cold as when you begin to recall the fires of home.[7]

It Would Be Nice, But…

What I've been describing is, of course, a somewhat idealized concept of congregational fellowship. Even within churches where genuine fellowship exists, there are always different levels of fellowship and always people who experience that fellowship in different ways. For example, some members consistently remain on the fringes of fellowship because that's where they choose to remain, due either to lack of commitment or understanding of the meaning of discipleship and Christian community. In other cases various circumstances may make it more difficult for some to en-

---

[7] White and Blue, 106.

gage fully in the life of the church. There will always be those who are new in Christ or new to a particular congregation and won't have been fully assimilated, at least not yet. Does this mean that discipline cannot be undertaken until we attain an ideal state of fellowship that involves everyone at the same level? Or does it suggest that those on the fringes shouldn't be subjected to congregational discipline when it would otherwise seem necessary?

The answer to both questions is certainly "No." The churches about which we read in the New Testament weren't perfect in fellowship any more than are churches today. The idea of a pristine state of early Christianity where everyone was fully committed to Christ and churches functioned just as they should is a myth and does not at all reflect what we read in the New Testament. The evidence shows that those churches had more than their share of problems, too. The controversy between "Hebrews and Hellenists" in Acts 6 and Paul's correspondence with the church at Corinth bear ample testimony to the reality of fellowship difficulties within early churches, yet those same churches were instructed to practice discipline. Likewise, discipline may sometimes be necessary in order to bring those on the fringes of the church closer to the center of God's will or to prevent their leaving the church entirely. What is essential here is not the perfection of our fellowship but the recognition that we must strive continually for a more perfect fellowship and that only when we care about one another can discipline do what God intends it to do.

So what if the leaders of a church realize that they haven't been doing what God requires and what is needed in regard to discipline? Where should you begin in order to correct the situation? My suggestion is to strive to create an environment of love and fellowship, "a church flaming with true koinonia," as White and Blue put it. Don't even think about taking disciplinary action (especially withdrawal of fellowship), but consider ways to increase and enhance fellowship and promote a spirit of love and concern among the members. So often churches start with a list of names out of the past and try to figure out how to rectify their neglect in not disciplining them. But it's far better to start with the people you have now and with whom you are in weekly contact. Disciplinary acts in the present cannot erase our fellowship failures of the past, so don't even try. Rather, encourage genuine participation in one another's lives, true pastoral concern on the part of the church's shepherds, real service to one another, the teaching of the truth in love, and a spirit of concern for each other in good times and in bad—including when sin arises. *Intensive fellowship must precede intensive discipline, or else it will be nothing but destructive.*

So rather than simply recognizing our lack of congregational discipline, we must see the larger problem: lack of congregational fellowship. If we work to correct the more basic problem, then effective, godly discipline can and will occur in our churches. In fact, it will become the norm simply because people care so much about one another that they can't sit by and do nothing when sin is taking its toll in the life of a fellow believer.

For Thought and Discussion

1. Have you personally witnessed situations where discipline was administered apart from fellowship? What was the outcome? How could it have been prevented?

2. On a scale of one to ten, how would you rate the level of spiritual fellowship in the congregation where you worship? Compare your response to that of others within the church. If there are differences in your responses, why do you think they exist?

3. What could your church do to improve the level and quality of

its fellowship? What could you do personally?

4. In what sense does discipline express fellowship? Why can there be no true fellowship if there is no willingness to discipline one another?

5. Considering the terms "excommunicate" and "disfellowship," which do you think is preferable for general use in churches today? Are there reasons to prefer one over the other? If so, what are they? Can you think of other terms that might be more helpful?

FIVE

Speaking the Truth in Love
Ephesians 4.15–16

Truth is not only violated by falsehood; it may be equally out-
raged by silence. (Henri Amiel)

Ephesians 4 contains Paul's well known appeal for the church to
"maintain the unity of the Spirit in the bond of peace." He has
demonstrated in chapters 1 through 3 that the unity of the church
is built in by God, that the "mystery"—the plan of God from
before the foundation of the world—is that all humanity should
be united in one body, the church. Therefore the church is not
called upon to *create* unity; God has already done that. Our task
is simply to *maintain* unity—that is, to do all we can to promote
it and not do anything that might destroy it. This is the only way
we can "walk in a manner worthy of the calling to which you have
been called" (4.1).

As a basis for his appeal Paul reminds us of the essentials of
faith which make us one in Christ: one body, one Spirit, one hope,
one Lord, one faith, one baptism, one God (vv 4–6). Yet within
that unity there is a marvelous diversity of gifts[1] that enable peo-

---

[1] In this context, Paul has in mind particularly gifts of leadership. For other kinds of
gifts, see Romans 12.6–8 and 1 Peter 4.10–11, in addition to the miraculous gifts of the
Spirit listed in 1 Corinthians 12.

ple of various talents and strengths to function as a unit for the good of the whole and to the glory of God. So Paul reminds us of that diversity in verses 5–14. Then in verses 15–16 he challenges us to maintain a balance in our church life, which is often difficult for Christians to achieve—the balance between truth and love:

> Rather, speaking the truth in love, we are to grow up in every way into him who is the head, into Christ, from whom the whole body, joined and held together by every joint with which it is equipped, when each part is working properly, makes the body grow so that it builds itself up in love.

As most of us know from painful experience, it is easy to speak the truth without love, but such truthfulness can be brutal and destructive. On the other hand, there are people who think they can love others without telling them the truth, even when they desperately need it. Such "love" is an illusion, a mere sentimentality. But when Christians practice "speaking the truth in love," Paul says wonderful results occur: the church is spiritually healthier, we grow into the likeness of Christ, who is the embodiment of truth in love, and we move on to maturity and growth. Perhaps this explains why so many churches never attain the kind of church life which Paul describes, why, in spite of using all the techniques of church growth, most churches still don't grow. Maybe our problem is, in part at least, an absence of the practice of "truth in love." And as we will see, what we call "church discipline" plays a vital role in maintaining the balance between truth and love.

What Is "Truth"?

First we need to ask, what kind of "truth" is Paul talking about? The usual understanding of verses 14–15 is that Paul is calling for a mutual confession of the same *doctrinal* truth. This fits well in the context, since in verse 14 he says we need to grow past the stage of being children, "tossed to and fro by the waves and carried about by every wind of doctrine." There's no doubt that speaking the truth in love has a great deal to do with sharing a common understanding of doctrine, since it's impossible to have unity if there is disagreement on the fundamental issues Paul outlines in verses 4–6. This is consistent with Paul's own practice in his ministry, since he proclaims, "we have renounced disgraceful, underhanded ways. We refuse to practice cunning or to tamper with God's word, but by the open statement of the truth we would commend ourselves to everyone's conscience in the sight of God" (2 Cor 4.2). This truth which Paul proclaimed so openly was obviously the gospel, and a common commitment to such truth is essential to the maintenance of unity and fellowship. But this open statement of doctrinal truth must be done considerately, not without regard to the impact of truth on people. Even "hard" truths can be said lovingly.

But it seems unlikely that doctrinal truth is all that Paul has in mind in these verses, since a common adherence to specific doctrines will not by itself bring about the kind of unity he describes. Mere conformity to doctrinal norms is not the same as unity of spirit and purpose, as the existence of many loveless and lifeless but "doctrinally sound" churches attests. There is a corresponding need for what we might call "personal truth."[2] The word which most English translations render as "speaking the truth" (*aletheuo*) doesn't necessarily refer only to speaking. Truth is more than mere verbal accuracy, and this word includes both "speaking the truth"

---

[2] I do not mean by this expression what is often meant by it, that there is no general or universal truth, and that truth is only true as far as the individual perceives it. Rather, I mean truth about ourselves, basic honesty.

and "dealing truly,"[3] "being utterly genuine, sincere, and honest."[4] This understanding of being truthful also fits well in the context of Ephesians 4.15, since in the previous verse Paul mentioned cunning, craftiness, and deceit as truth's opposites. Christians, by contrast, are to be genuine, truthful people. In today's language, Paul says we need to "be real" with each other both in our speech and in our actions.

Several verses later, in 4.25, personal truth is clearly Paul's concern: "Therefore, having put away falsehood, let each one of you speak the truth with his neighbor, for we are members one of another." Notice that here the motive for being truthful with one another is our *fellowship*. Being untruthful with each other is the surest way to destroy or prevent fellowship. People who will not "be real" with each other can never enjoy real spiritual unity, and being untruthful is one of the most un-Christian things we can do. According to Colossians 3.9–10, being untruthful is part of the "old life" which should have been put away at conversion: "Do not lie to one another, seeing that you have put off the old self with its practices and have put on the new self, which is being renewed in knowledge after the image of its creator." Being untruthful with one another is simply not in harmony with the image of God, who is Himself the embodiment of all truth, that image into which we are supposed to be transformed.

Being Truthful About You and Me

Taking this discussion a step further, there are two aspects of personal truth (being real) which are essential to fellowship. The

---

[3] Francis Foulkes, *The Epistle of Paul to the Ephesians* (Grand Rapids: Eerdmans, 1963), 123. For another example of the ambiguity of *aletheuo* see Gal 4.16: "Have I then become your enemy by telling you the truth?" The ESV marginal note offers as an alternative: "by dealing truthfully with you."

[4] C.L. Mitton, *New Century Bible Commentary: Ephesians* (Grand Rapids: Eerdmans, 1973), 156.

first is being individually truthful about ourselves. We must be willing to confess our own neediness, our struggles, our problems, even our sins. We aren't called together as the body of Christ because we are paragons of righteousness, not because we're "okay" and need simply to serve as examples for others to emulate. Rather, we are called together in Christ precisely because in and of ourselves we *aren't* okay. And because we aren't, we need the Lord and each other. But in many churches, such honesty about self either seldom occurs or is either directly or indirectly discouraged. Few of us want to allow others to see us as we really are. What would people think if they knew the truth about our marriages? Our children? Our temptations? Our failures? Our doubts? Our fears? And so we hide our real selves and then wonder why we feel so empty, so alone, even in the midst of the family of God. This is tragic because the very truthfulness we so studiously avoid has the power to set us free. When the woman with the flow of blood touched the hem of Jesus' garment, she did so secretly because she knew she was unclean and that her action was socially and religiously unacceptable. But when Jesus called her out, she "came in fear and trembling and fell down before him, and *told him the whole truth*" (Mark 5.33). And in that full confession she found liberation and healing, since Jesus told her to "be healed" of her infirmity. In the same way, a great deal of healing can take place in our lives when we are willing to be honest about ourselves in the presence of our brothers and sisters in Christ.[5]

---

[5] What I am advocating here is a basic honesty with one another, but not the practice of "letting it all hang out" with everyone at church and in any Christian gathering. Not everyone is spiritually mature enough to handle the sensitive information we might need to confess. Some could be harmed by hearing it, while others might be tempted to gossip. So we need to use good judgment about when, where, and to whom we open up concerning our needs and struggles. James' admonition to "confess your sins to one another and pray for one another, that you may be healed" (Jas 5.16) does not require that we do so before the whole church. Using such judgment about when and to whom we confess our needs and sins is not the same thing as being untruthful with one another.

The other aspect of personal truth that we urgently need in our churches is truthfulness about each other. There are times when we need to confront one another lovingly about our actions and attitudes in order to help each other see the reality of what is going on in our lives. Jesus taught, "If you brother sins against you, go and tell him his fault between you and him alone" (Matt 18.15)[6]. How often does this actually happen in most churches, where people tend to bend over backward to be polite and not offend one another or where we prefer to practice avoidance of the unpleasant rather than loving confrontation? As a result a great deal of fellowship is disrupted or never develops because of offenses, misunderstandings, and miscommunications that could have been resolved simply by "being real" with each other. When Jesus taught us to go to our offending brother, it was simply another way of saying, "Speak the truth in love."

Running the Risk of Truthfulness

Most of us find such truth-telling as Jesus describes difficult, but it's no less necessary. We find it so hard simply because of our fear. I may fear what others will think of me if they know the truth about me. Will I find understanding or help? Will I become the subject of gossip? We all rightly fear alienating or offending others if we approach them about problems in their lives, no matter how lovingly we may do so. Some people simply don't want to hear the truth and will take offense. Paul knew that risk well. After scolding the Galatian churches for abandoning their trust in Christ in favor of reliance on the law (especially circumcision), he asks, "Have I then become your enemy by telling you the truth?" (Gal 4.16). There is an old Slavic proverb which says, "Tell the truth—and run!"

---

[6]Jesus' words are further evidence of the point made in note 5. Private conversation is sometimes preferable to public airing of our concerns.

Part of our fear when it comes to confronting others is the possibility of causing a problem within the congregation with whom we worship. No one wants to be the source of trouble in the church. But we often forget that sin itself—not honesty about sin—is the worst form of trouble we can have. Jesus once proclaimed that His enemies wanted to kill Him precisely because He had told them the truth about themselves (John 8.45). Truth-telling can be risky business, but the reality is that love is *always* risky. When we speak truthfully with someone, we run the risk of being rejected or becoming the object of their recriminations, so it's easier just to keep quiet. Yet over and over again the Scriptures teach us to speak the truth. When Jesus encountered the Samaritan woman at the well (John 4), He didn't allow her to avoid the truth about her spiritual condition as revealed in her sad marital history. His goal in probing the subject of her marriages wasn't to embarrass her or to cause pain but to draw her out where she could face the truth about her life. Once He had done so, she was ready to hear His message about the "living water," but it took a confrontation with the truth to get her to realize her need, much less act on it.

Paul instructed the Thessalonians to "respect those who labor among you and are over you in the Lord and admonish you" (1 Thess 5.12). Two verses later he exhorted them to "admonish the idle, encourage the fainthearted, help the weak, be patient with them all." To "admonish" someone means to warn, advise, remind, teach, and spur them on to better conduct.[7] Far from being an exceptional activity in the life of the church, Paul indicates that it should be the norm. In encouraging Timothy to fulfill his ministry, Paul charged him to "reprove, rebuke, and exhort" (2 Tim 4.2). Likewise he tells Titus to "rebuke ... sharply" the Cre-

---

[7] F. Selter, "Exhort, etc.," *The New International Dictionary of New Testament Theology*, Vol. 1 (Grand Rapids: Zondervan, 1975), 567.

tan false teachers and to admonish only "once and then twice" the divisive man before avoiding him completely (Tit 1.13, 3.10–11). Even elders who "persist in sin" are to be rebuked "in the presence of all" (1 Tim 5.20). It's clear that Paul took truth-telling seriously as part of the ongoing life of the church.

In other words, we all have our failings, but that doesn't mean they are to be ignored when we see them gaining a foothold in one another's lives or when they are creating problems for the body as a whole. Rather, we are to confront these people and situations truthfully and lovingly so that the necessary corrections can be made. This, too, is a form of discipline, one which, if practiced more consistently than is usually the case, would prevent many bad situations from becoming worse. Where Christians regularly speak the truth in love to one another, discipline will occur naturally and spontaneously, because speaking the truth in love *is* discipline or at least the beginnings of it.

Truthfulness *vs.* Pretense

The opposite of the kind of truth-telling I have described above is not lying but *pretense*. When we aren't truthful with each other, we pretend all is well, even though we know it isn't. And nothing is more damaging to real fellowship than pretense. Pretending I'm okay, even though deep inside I'm hurting and needing help. Pretending there is no sin in my brother or sister's life when it's obvious to all that there is. Pretending that someone's ugly, divisive attitude isn't doing any harm to the body of Christ, when in reality it's poisoning the life of the entire congregation. Pretending to be friends with people we really resent because of offenses or misunderstandings we're simply unwilling to address. Where practices such as these exist, real fellowship cannot. And to speak of "fellowship" without truth-telling makes a sham of the entire concept.

"Speak the truth in love." "Put away falsehood." "Let us speak the truth with our neighbor, for we are members one of another." In all of these ways the Bible charges us to "be real" with each other. By openly declaring the gospel truths which make us one body in Christ, by confessing our weaknesses and struggles and sins and therefore our need for Christ and each other, and by lovingly confronting each other about sin whenever necessary, we contribute to the growth of the church in love so that it will "grow up in every way into him who is the head, into Christ," so that it "builds itself up in love."

It isn't easy, but it's worth it!

For Thought and Discussion

1. What happens in a church when the truth is spoken without love? What happens when there is "love" (emotionally) but no speaking of the truth?

2. What are some ways in which Christians sometimes fail to deal truthfully with one another?

3. Why do you think we are often reluctant to "be real" with one another? What can we (you) do to correct this situation?

4. How can truth-telling sometimes be risky business? Can you think of biblical examples of people who brought trouble on themselves by telling the truth? Does that mean they shouldn't have done it?

5. Explain in your own words why pretense damages fellowship.

SIX

I *Am* My Brother's Keeper
Matthew 18.15–17

A disciplining church will prove more loving in the long run than a church that advertises God's love but then shows no interest in whether this love is practiced by her members. ... A church that disciples people into an undisciplined church lives a lie. Integrity requires both inner and outer mission. (F.D. Bruner, *Matthew: A Commentary*)

When God questioned Cain concerning the whereabouts of his murdered brother, Cain responded defiantly, "I do not know; am I my brother's keeper?" (Gen 4.9). Although Cain's motive was evil, his question was a good one, and it's one we ought to ask as well: *"Am* I my brother's keeper?" To what extent am I responsible for you and you for me and for the person who sits next to both of us on the pew each Sunday morning? Is there a line of privacy that limits my involvement in the spiritual life of my brother or sister, or do I have an obligation to watch over them to the extent that I am able?

In Genesis 4 the answer to this question was a resounding "Yes!" Cain *was* responsible for what happened to his brother (especially since he had killed him!)—and so are we, even more so in the kingdom of God. Because we are God's children and brothers and sisters to one another, we are our brother's keeper. But note: this isn't the same thing as saying we are our brother's *manipulator.* In some so-called "discipling" churches the practice is for members to ride herd on one another's spirituality, even to the point of telling them where they can and can't work, who they can and can't date, etc., and threatening them with ostracism if they don't comply. This is a complete distortion of the biblical model of the church. Still, there is a legitimate sphere of spiritual responsibility for one another's welfare, and this is Jesus' concern in Matthew 18.15–17. In this chapter and the next we'll take a closer look at this important text in order to see what that responsibility entails.

> If your brother sins, go and point it out to him between you and him alone. If he listens to you, you have gained your brother. But if he does not listen, take with you one or two others so that by the testimony of two or three witnesses every word may be confirmed. But if he does not listen to them, tell it to the church; and if he does not listen even to the church, let him be to you as a Gentile and a tax collector. (my translation)

Matthew 18.15–17 in Context

It's impossible to over-estimate the importance of Matthew 18.15–17 for the study of godly church discipline. Not only does it come from the lips of Jesus Himself, it is also the most comprehensive of all New Testament texts on the subject, since it covers the big picture from offense to loving confrontation to withdrawal and forgiveness. Likewise, along with Galatians 6.1 (which we'll discuss later), it is the most general text on discipline because it discusses sins in general rather than specific cases or types of sin. Since it expresses the foundational principle on which later New Testament statements[1] about discipline are based, it's important that we understand it thoroughly. To do this we must begin with a good grasp of the context in which these words occur in Matthew's Gospel.

The basic structure of Matthew is rather simple: it alternates blocks of narrative (story) with large sections of teaching material. There are five such teaching sections in Matthew, and these are frequently called the "five great discourses." They include the Sermon on the Mount (chs 5–7); Jesus' instructions to the Twelve as He sent them out to proclaim the kingdom (ch 10); parables of the kingdom (ch 13); and the "eschatological discourse" in which Jesus spoke of the coming destruction of Jerusalem and the eventual coming of the Son of Man (chs 24–25). Matthew 18 is the fourth of these five discourses, and its theme is "Kingdom Relationships." The first verses of chapters 18 and 19 bracket the section as a connected series of instructions ("At that time"—18.1; "Now when Jesus had finished these sayings"—19.1), and the contents suggest there is one overall theme. Chapter 18 explains how followers of Jesus, beginning with the apostles but not limited to them, are to interact with and treat one another. The communal nature of this section is highlighted by the fact that this is one of only two places in Matthew where the word "church" (*ekklesia*) occurs (18.17; the other is 16.18) and that Matthew is the only one of the four Gospels to contain this word. Jesus apparently realized that one of the greatest challenges confronting the new communities of His followers would be in the personal realm: how to get along with one another and help one another attain the spiritual goals He laid out for us. "Within such a community

---

[1] Keep in mind that the "later" statements, such as those of Paul, were probably written down before Jesus' words were written. There can be little question, however, that Jesus' teachings were already widely known in their oral form and influenced what was eventually written in the New Testament letters.

there is opportunity both to harm and to care for others, and the health and effectiveness of the group will depend on the attitudes to one another which are fostered."[2]

"Who's the Greatest?"

Jesus' words on the subject of discipline occur about the middle of the chapter, so let's back up and see how it all begins. Interestingly, it begins with a conflict among the disciples: "At that time the disciples came to Jesus saying, 'Who is the greatest in the kingdom of heaven?'" A careful reading of the Synoptic Gospels reveals that the disciples asked this question not in a general way but about themselves: "Which *of us* is the greatest?" Likewise, we should note that this was far from the only time they discussed this subject. Mark 9.33–37 relates an incident when Jesus asked them, "What were you discussing on the way?" They were too embarrassed to tell Him, "for on the way they had argued with one another about who was the greatest." This was all the more remarkable, since Jesus had just predicted for the second time His own impending suffering, death, and resurrection (9.30–32). Then there was the time when the mother of James and John came to Jesus and asked Him to give her sons the most prominent positions in his coming kingdom.[3] After Jesus informed both mother and sons that such a request was not His to grant, Matthew tells us that the other ten disciples became indignant when they heard it (Matt 20.24). Apparently they coveted these choice places for themselves and were perturbed that the two brothers had beaten them to the punch. Luke relates that even in the midst of the Last Supper, as Jesus

---

[2] R.T. France, *The Gospel According to Matthew* (Grand Rapids: Eerdmans, 1985), 269.

[3] Underlying this request was an obvious misconception of Jesus' kingdom, that it was to be a political/military establishment. Mrs. Zebedee wanted her two boys to occupy key positions of power and authority in it.

spoke of His approaching betrayal and death, "A dispute also arose among them, as to which of them was to be regarded as the greatest" (Luke 22.24).[4] Clearly, the desire for prominence and power in the kingdom is nothing new, nor, unfortunately, has it gotten much better after two thousand years.[5]

Back to Matthew 18: Jesus responds by presenting a child—not a general or cabinet member or CEO—as the model for them to emulate. They must "turn and become like children" in order even to be *in* His kingdom, and "Whoever humbles himself like this child is the greatest in the kingdom of heaven" (18.2–4). Obviously the standards of greatness in Jesus' kingdom were going to be far different than in the world at large. The point of the child model is not innocence, as is often claimed. Rather, as stated in verse 4, the supreme virtue is humility, but in a particular sense. Children in ancient Jewish society were objects of great affection, but they had absolutely no status, no "rights" beyond what the adults in their lives extended to them.[6] So what is Jesus saying? That His disciples must empty themselves of the desire for status and power; such is true greatness in the kingdom of Him who emptied Himself of all privilege in order to be our Savior (see Phil 2.5–11).

---

[4] It was probably this disputing at the table which prompted Jesus to arise and wash the disciples' feet as a lesson in humility and service, as recorded in John 13.

[5] C.E.B. Cranfield says, "the question of precedence was specially important in Palestine and was incessantly arising, whether in the synagogue service or judicial proceedings or at meals" (*The Gospel According to Saint Mark* [Cambridge: University Press, 1966], 34).

[6] "In modern Western societies children are often seen as very important, but in first-century Judaism they were not. ... In the affairs of men children were unimportant. They could not fight, they could not lead, they had not had time to acquire worldly wisdom, they could not pile up riches, they counted for very little. To speak of them as humble is surely a reference to their small size rather than any intellectual or spiritual virtue. Their smallness made them very humble members of society" (Leon Morris, *The Gospel According to Matthew* [Grand Rapids: Eerdmans, 1992], 60).

Caring for All, Discounting None

The next section of the discourse (vv 5–11) continues the theme of child-likeness and the willingness of disciples to accept all other disciples, regardless of their apparent insignificance. Jesus expresses His concern that disciples "receive" *all* of His "little ones" (believers—v 6) and that they not cause them to sin either through direct temptation or by refusing to accept them and thus pushing them outside the community. "Receive" in this context means to "accept as infinitely valuable."[7] Jesus warns the disciples not to "despise" (look down upon, count as of no value) one of these little ones, because even the most insignificant has angelic representation in heaven and is deeply cared for by "my Father who is in heaven" (vv 10–11). Not only was this a rebuke to the Twelve, it is equally so to churches in our own time, in which some members are considered as of less importance than others and are allowed to fall through the cracks with little effort to reclaim them. As Douglas Hare writes, "How easy it is for the active members of a church to ignore those who play no leadership role and contribute only modestly to the budget!"[8]

Jesus then gives a memorable illustration of this concern for all of His followers in the Parable of the Lost Sheep (vv 12–14). Since these verses immediately precede Jesus' words about discipline, they are of great importance for our discussion. It's important to note that the point of this parable is not, as is often supposed, to demonstrate that Jesus (or God) is the Good Shepherd who cares for every one of His sheep. While that is the point of the Lost Sheep parable in the context of Luke 15, that isn't the case here. True, God is concerned for the welfare of each of His sheep, but this context points out that going after the lost sheep

---

[7] Douglas R. A. Hare, *Matthew* (Louisville: John Knox, 1993), 211.

[8] Hare, 212.

is the responsibility of the church: "See that *you* do not despise one of these little ones." The Good Shepherd motif represents the concern that Jesus expects every believer to have for every other believer. In this sense we are to be "keepers" of one another. The shepherd's unwillingness to simply write off even one sheep shows that everyone in the kingdom is important to God (v 14) and so must be to us. In the kingdom of God we have no right to discount or disregard the worth of anyone. No one is dispensable. We are no more permitted to disregard our brother than we are to cause him to sin (vv 7–9). "So it is not the will of my Father who is in heaven that one of these little ones should perish."

Generally speaking, our modern neglect in this regard is painfully obvious. How often does it happen in churches that people just disappear without notice? We speak of "fringe members" and people who "fall through the cracks" as though such things were the norm and need not concern us unduly,[9] although Jesus says it should never happen. We should be able to account for every sheep, because every one belongs to God and is of inestimable value. Perhaps the first step in restoring godly discipline in the church ought to be repentance over our indifference toward so many of God's sheep. While this is a primary responsibility of elders, as we shall see later, it is also the responsibility of every disciple.

Therefore...

It is this emphatic teaching about congregational concern for the individual which leads to Jesus' words about disciplining those who sin. It is essential that we keep this context firmly

---

[9] F.D. Bruner gives a penetrating example of one way this sometimes happens when he writes, "The temptation for the spiritually serious is to look down on half-hearted or 'nominal' Christians, on people to whom Jesus Christ seems to mean too little. Fourth-soil Christians find it hard to like the other three soils" (*Matthew*, Vol. 2 [Dallas: Word, 1990], 641).

in mind, so that we cease to think of verses 15–17 as simply outlining a "disciplinary procedure." Rather, we must recognize them as describing *a means of regaining those who become lost*, for preserving erring disciples intact within the Christian family in spite of their sin. The steps outlined in verses 15–17 are the Christ-ordained way of refusing to allow people to disappear from the church as if they were never among us, even when they may have personally wronged us.

The remainder of chapter 18 continues the theme of infinite concern, with Peter's question about how often he must forgive his brother (vv 21–22) and Jesus' reply: as often as necessary. This point is then reinforced with the Parable of the Unmerciful Servant (vv 23–25), one of Jesus' most powerful stories. Its lesson is clear: "Don't you *dare* drive anyone out of the kingdom by refusing to forgive them!"

So the message of the entire eighteenth chapter is a rebuke to the spirit of self-seeking and self-serving and emphasizes that in Jesus' kingdom everyone is important, no matter how insignificant they are from a worldly perspective. And every member of the kingdom is required to be concerned for the spiritual welfare of every other member, even to the point of personal confrontation about sin. No one is expendable.[10]

With this principle firmly in mind, in the next chapter we turn to a close examination of Jesus' instructions.

---

[10] "In a formally constituted church with an appointed leadership, it is easy for the 'ordinary' disciple to hide behind that authority structure and to leave it all to the official leaders, appealing to Cain's question 'Am I my brother's keeper?' with the comfortable assumption that the answer must be No. But this passage asserts that the answer is Yes. In a community of 'little ones,' each must be concerned about and take responsibility for the spiritual welfare of the other" (R. T. France, *The Gospel of Matthew* [Grand Rapids, MI and Cambridge, U.K., 2007], 691–92).

For Thought and Discussion

1. What aspects of American culture encourage us to feel that we are *not* our brother's keeper?

2. Explain why Matthew 18.15–17 is such an important text in the discussion of church discipline.

3. How does the disciples' question about "who is the greatest" fit into the context of Matthew 18?

4. How many people are on the "membership roll" of the church with whom you worship whose presence cannot be accounted for? How and why does this happen? What can be done to correct this situation?

5. Are there members of your congregation who could easily slip through the cracks through the neglect of others? Why? What can/should be done to prevent this from happening?

SEVEN

What to do When Your Brother Sins

Matthew 18.15–17

My brothers, if anyone among you wanders from the truth and someone brings him back, let him know that whoever brings back a sinner from his wandering will save his soul from death and will cover a multitude of sins. (James 5.19–20)

Now let's take a closer look at Jesus' specific instructions about reclaiming a brother[1] who deviates into sin. Because this text is vital to our understanding of discipline and because the context is so important for understanding this text, please be sure you have read the preceding chapter before beginning this one.

"If Your Brother Sins..."

Jesus begins, "if your brother sins..." (v 15). He leaves us in no doubt that people in God's kingdom sometimes sin and that we

---

[1] No apology is necessary for retaining Jesus' use of the masculine reference, while recognizing that His words apply equally to both sexes. As noted previously, the New Revised Standard Version seriously blurs the fellowship aspect of Jesus' words by translating *adelphos* ("brother") as "another member of the church" and "that one" in verse 15, and by using "the member," "the offender," and "such a one" in place of the masculine pronoun in verses 15–17. Not only does this obscure the concept of fellowship in this text but it is unnecessary and creates a clumsy translation of an otherwise straightforward paragraph.

must take sin seriously and can never simply ignore it. We can scarcely deny that today's church seldom takes sin as seriously as Jesus says we should. Perhaps it is our American "live and let live" mentality, our sense of rugged individualism, the cultural sanctity of minding one's own business, or the concept that nothing is universally "sinful." Whatever the cause, we must confess a spiritual insensitivity to sin.[2] We don't want to acknowledge it in ourselves, and it is much easier simply to let it slide in the lives of others. But to do so is to fail to take seriously the destructive nature of sin, and Jesus won't allow us this luxury.

Note that Jesus speaks of our "brother's" sin. Some commentators see a shift at this point from the discussion about Jesus' "little ones" earlier in the chapter to matters concerning one's "brother."[3] But this misses the point of Matthew 18 entirely, because it destroys the unity of thought in the discourse. Our "brother" *is* one of Jesus' "little ones" and is not to be despised, sinned against, ignored, or left to perish in his sin. Our relationship as fellow-citizens of Christ's kingdom requires action in the event of a brother's sin.

An important question arises at this point regarding v 15: Did Jesus say, "If your brother sins" or "if your brother sins *against you*"? The words "against you" are present in most of the ancient Greek manuscripts, but they are missing in some important ones. The various English translations reflect this reality. The King James, English Standard, Revised Standard, New Revised Standard,

---

[2] "Setting right other adults fits awkwardly into contemporary Western culture with its postmodern tendencies, but it plays an important part in the NT and fits comfortably into the larger Jewish frame" (John Nolland, *The Gospel of Matthew: A Commentary on the Greek Text* [Grand Rapids, MI and Cambridge, U.K.: William B. Eerdmans Publishing Company, 2005], 746).

[3] See, for example, W.D. Davies and Dale C. Allison, Jr., *A Critical and Exegetical Commentary on the Gospel According to Saint Matthew*, Vol. II (Edinburgh: T & T Clark, 1991), 750–751; and Daniel J. Harrington, *The Gospel of Matthew* (Collegeville, Minn.: The Liturgical Press, 1991), 265.

New International, and Today's English versions, along with J. B. Phillips' paraphrase-translation, include the phrase, though some of them have notes indicating the variation. The New American Standard Bible, Jerusalem Bible, New English Bible, and Revised English Bible omit it. Commentaries are fairly evenly divided on the question, with perhaps a slight majority favoring the omission of "against you."[4] If the words were not originally in Matthew's text, they were probably added by a later scribe who was familiar with the parallel in Luke 17.4: "...and if he sins against you seven times in the day, and turns to you seven times, saying, 'I repent,' you must forgive him."[5] Likewise Peter's question in Matthew 18.21 ("how often will my brother sin against me, and I forgive him?") might suggest that a personal offense is under consideration in verse 15, and this could have influenced an early copyist to add "against you." On the whole it seems best to omit "against you," but this must be said with caution.[6]

Does it make any difference? Possibly a great deal. Some conclude that Jesus' words and the obligation to confront the sinner personally apply only if the offense is personal in nature. So if the sin is not "against me," they reason, then I am excused from the requirement to go to the sinning brother and am permitted to discuss his sin with others rather than with him. This assertion frequently arises when someone has concluded that a brother is a false teacher; since false teaching isn't a personal offense, the ac-

---

[4] B.M. Metzger in *A Textual Commentary on the Greek New Testament* categorizes the variation as having a "considerable degree of doubt" about which reading is correct (United Bible Societies, 1971), 45.

[5] Luke 17.4 is a close parallel to Matthew 18.15–17 and should be studied in combination with it. The passage in Luke seems to be something of a capsule summary of the Matthean text and emphasizes likewise the concern for not causing others to sin in the context of an overall pattern of Christian relationships.

[6] France (2007) says the reference is to sin in general, not to personal injury, so "to speak of 'grievance' or 'conflict resolution' here is inappropriate" (692).

cuser then feels at liberty to openly criticize the accused to others. Such an attitude clearly violates the spirit of this text and of its context and often becomes an excuse for not confronting someone with whom we disagree. As we will see later, Paul takes a different stance toward outside agitators than toward those who are inside the Christian community, but never does he suggest that any brother is unworthy of our efforts to reclaim him or that the label "false teacher" is license to kill verbally. (See Titus 3.10–11 for a pertinent example. Even the perversely divisive are to be warned.)[7] Even if the words "against you" are judged to be original, this does not excuse any of us from failing to approach a brother or sister who is involved in sin—any sin, even false teaching. Bound together in the Christian fellowship as we are, there is a sense in which *all* sin is "against me." But the primary thrust of Jesus' words is not toward determining who is offended but reclaiming the offender. We shouldn't quibble about words when people's reputations and souls are at stake.[8]

---

[7] It should be observed that although Paul frequently speaks out boldly against false teachings and teachers, only rarely does he mention people by name. This may be due to the fact that his readers already knew about whom he was speaking. It may also be a deliberate attempt to keep attention focused on the error rather than creating a clash over personalities, and to avoid sinning against brothers whom he had not had the opportunity to confront personally. First Timothy 1.18–20 and 2 Timothy 4.14–15 are exceptions to Paul's general practice, and in both instances Paul has had personal confrontations with the people named. In other cases he speaks quite harshly about false teachers and opponents without naming them, even though he apparently knows who they are. See, for example, Philippians 3.2ff, Romans 3.8, 2 Corinthians 10.10–12, 11.12–15.

[8] See, for example, Galatians 6.1, which specifies that "any sin" in which a brother is overtaken demands our efforts at restoration. G.W.H. Lampe argues that it is clear that Matthew 18.15–17 is not dealing only with personal offenses, because these are dealt with in 18.21ff "by the very different method of unlimited forgiveness" ("Church Discipline and the Interpretation of the Epistles to the Corinthians," in *Christian History and Interpretation: Studies Presented to John Knox*, ed. W.R. Farmer *et al* [Cambridge: University Press, 1967], 345).

But *Which* Sins?

A somewhat troubling aspect of this passage is that Jesus doesn't specify precisely what sins or kinds of sins require our attention. Are we expected to approach every brother or sister about every mistake we might see in his or her life? If not, at what point should one believer intervene in the life of another regarding his or her sin?

A frequent answer to this question is that we should intervene if the sin is of a public nature, that is, if it is something known generally among the congregation as well as in the community. In this case discipline is understood primarily as a way of salvaging the church's reputation. But Jesus didn't say, "If your brother sins *publicly* go and tell him his fault," so this seems to be a questionable conclusion. Likewise, the concern for privacy expressed in verse 15 would seem to rule out public knowledge as either the sole or even the primary criterion for deciding when we should act.

Others suggest that, before we are required to act, the sin must be determined to be both serious and intentional, but this finds little, if any, support in the text.[9] Galatians 6.1 specifies that we should seek to restore a brother who is "overtaken in (or by) *any* sin," so perhaps we should be cautious in trying to delineate too sharply which sins require action on our part and which do not.

At the risk of saying more than Jesus said, I would like to suggest some criteria for deciding when to "go to a brother."

1. *The seriousness of a particular sin.* While it's certainly true that "a sin is a sin," it is equally true that not all sins are equal in their impact on the sinner, the church, and the watching community. (See 1 Corinthians 5, for example.) Being unfaithful to

---

[9] This is the view of Davies and Allison (782). Even wider of the mark is the claim of Daniel J. Harrington that "The biblical procedure presupposes a criminal offence, not a problem within a community" (269).

one's wife or husband is hardly in the same category as breaking the speed limit.[10]

2. *Whether someone has committed a "mistake," or is practicing sin habitually.* While a refusal to attend worship is a matter of concern even if it occurs once, the habitual "forsaking of the assembly" (Heb 10.25) would certainly demand attention.

3. *Sins which are grossly inconsistent with the Christian life.* This would include (but not be limited to) such sins as sexual immorality, which Paul addresses in Ephesians 5 and Colossians 3.

4. *The impact of a particular sin on the church as a whole.* This consideration may impact not only whether or not to act but also with what degree of urgency.

These are certainly not hard-and-fast rules and are in no way intended to belittle the seriousness of any sin, but perhaps they will provide some guidelines for deciding whether or not to initiate disciplinary action. Also, in the following chapters we will encounter texts which speak of specific sins requiring discipline, and these are invaluable guides in making such determinations. If action is required by these Scriptures, then it is in all likelihood required under the same or similar circumstances now.

Deciding whether to confront someone about sin will inevitably be a matter of judgment and should always be approached in a prayerful and humble manner.[11]

---

[10] "Matthew's view of sin is strong in that it preserves us from that moral twilight in which all cats are gray, in which no sins are more serious than others, and so over which a mist of indifference can hang ('after all, we all sin')" (Bruner, 646).

[11] Jonathan Leeman offers the helpful suggestion that "Formal church discipline or excommunication is warranted when an individual seems to happily abide in known sin. There's no evidence that the Spirit is making him or her uncomfortable, other than the discomfort of getting caught. Rather, obedience to sin's desires is *characteristic*" (Leeman, *Church Discipline*, 50). Notice that, while helpful, Leeman's guidelines are also somewhat subjective, as are those expressed above.

"Go and Tell Him His Fault"

In a situation where sin becomes known to us, Jesus says we are to act in a very specific manner: "tell him his fault, between you and him alone." This is an extremely important first step in dealing with sin but one which is often ignored. Our tendency is either to do nothing at all about our brother or sister's sin or else to tell others about it. Seldom do we do exactly as Jesus says by going to the sinner privately. Jesus' teaching suggests that we should deal with the problem at the lowest possible level, by involving no more people than necessary. Why is this aura of privacy so important? For one thing, we may find that our information about or impression of our brother's behavior is incorrect or has been wrongly interpreted. In such a case it might do great harm to have told others before discussing it with the person in question. Likewise, if he is guilty of a particular sin, we should try to avoid embarrassing him unnecessarily in order to make repentance less traumatic; so again, the fewer people who know about the problem, the better.[12]

The verb *elenchein* in the phrase "tell him his fault" means to bring to light, expose, or point out something to someone, to reprove and correct. (See, for example, its use in Luke 3.19, 1 Cor 14.24, 2 Tim 4.2, and Tit 1.9.) It need not include strong rebuke or severe judgment but simply an exposure of guilt, done in such a way as to induce repentance.[13] This is a delicate task, as anyone

[12] Craig S. Keener points out that the ancient rabbis had much to say about forgiveness and "emphasized that reproof was to be private whenever possible...a sage could thus rule that publicly shaming one's fellow warrants exclusion from the coming age. ...The Dead Sea Scrolls also emphasize this sequence: private reproof, then before witnesses, and finally before the gathered assembly. ... Public admonition was reserved for the severest of circumstances..." (*Matthew* [Downers Grove, IL: InterVarsity Press, 1997], 288).

[13] William G. Thompson, *Matthew's Advice to a Divided Community* (Rome: Biblical Institute Press, 1970), 178. Such texts as Proverbs 3.12, Job 5.17, Hebrews 12.5, etc. "depict God as One who educates by correction" (F. Buchsel, "*elencho*, etc." *Theological*

who has ever tried it can attest, and it is best accomplished exactly as Jesus says: alone.

"If He Listens…"

Jesus immediately reminds us of the goal of going to our brother: to "gain" him. In the New Testament this term usually refers to material gain, but here it aptly expresses the goal of all remedial church discipline: to get back into the fold people who may have wandered out. And it reminds us of the spirit in which such an effort must be undertaken, one of hopeful expectation of winning back our brother, not of "telling him off" and/or "getting rid" of him. As Thomas Long puts it, "the whole process is focused on the restoration of the offender, not revenge for the offended. … The point is to regain the brother or sister, to make the flock whole again, to bring the wandering sheep back into the protection and care of the fold."[14] In other words, going to a sinning brother or sister is not simply the first step toward withdrawing fellowship from him or her. Each of the actions taught by Jesus is complete within itself and may be sufficient for regaining our brother or sister. We should, therefore, pursue each one as if it alone will be sufficient, not in anticipation of a negative outcome requiring further action.

"But If He Does Not Listen…"

Not surprisingly, people don't normally like to hear about their sins, even when they're clearly in the wrong and even when those pointing them out have the best of intentions. Even the kindest, most humble effort at reproving may meet with rejection rather than appreciation. Human nature tells us to give up at the point

---

Dictionary of the New Testament, One Volume edition, ed. G.W. Bromiley [Grand Rapids: Eerdmans, 1985], 222).

[14] Thomas G. Long, *Matthew* (Louisville: Westminster John Knox Press, 1997), 210.

our efforts are rebuffed, but Jesus tells us to press on. Our brother is too important for us simply to walk away after a first refusal. So we should seek reinforcements in continuing our efforts.

The instruction to take one or two others with us "that every charge may be established by the evidence of two or three witnesses"[15] is not as much of a "judicial" act as the word "witnesses" might suggest. Note the continued concern for privacy— just one or two witnesses, not as many as we can round up. And their function isn't to serve as "witnesses for the prosecution" but for the protection of both the offending brother and the one trying to reclaim him.[16] Quite often in such confrontations meanings can be twisted, intentions misinterpreted, and previous statements misquoted. The witnesses, who were not part of the initial meeting between the two parties, can add balance and offer guidance and judgment for the ongoing discussion. (This is especially important when the "sin" is indeed some sort of personal affront.) Also, in the event that the witnesses determine that the accused person is in the wrong, they can add their own appeal for repentance.[17] As the beginning of verse 17 suggests, the goal is still reclamation, not dismissal. The witnesses are "to deprive the sinner of the later excuse that his accuser is biased or pursuing a selfish goal, is reproving him unjustly or in anger. ... In a real sense, they are to be adduced *for* the sinner, rather than *against* him."[18]

---

[15] An idea evidently derived from Deuteronomy 19.15.

[16] "Every charge" (ESV) is literally "every word," as in the Revised Standard Version. The NIV has "every matter."

[17] Nolland thinks the witnesses are people who have independent knowledge of the offense committed, as well as being witnesses to the confrontation between the accuser and the accused (746–47). Michael J. Wilkins, on the other hand, maintains they are witnesses to the confrontation, not to the original offense (*Matthew: The NIV Application Commentary* [Grand Rapids, MI: Zondervan, 2004], 618). Wilkins' view must certainly be correct, since in the absence of additional witnesses to the sin, it would be impossible to proceed as Jesus directs.

[18] Victor C. Pfitzner, "Purified Community—Purified Sinner," *Australian Biblical*

"Tell It to the Church"

If repeated efforts at restoration fail, the circle of those involved must widen. Jesus says, "tell it to the church." Hopefully it won't go this far, but if it does we must not shrink from doing as Jesus instructs, in hope that the offender will listen to the combined voices of the entire church. "Telling it to the church" is not simply an announcement of a decision made by the elders or someone else. Rather it is a call to the entire congregation to become involved in the very serious task of restoring a brother before it's too late. Our Lord could not have more clearly emphasized the responsibility of every Christian to be involved in the disciplinary process. The whole church is to be active in discipline for the added effect of a united appeal. Also, in the unfortunate event that withdrawal of fellowship becomes necessary, everyone can own the decision. It is extremely important that this phase of the restoration process not be overlooked, otherwise considerable confusion and unrest may result among those who are uninformed as to why the decision was made. Withdrawing the church's fellowship is never the prerogative of a few but the responsibility of the entire body. Except in some extremely delicate cases, it is a decision that should be made *by* the church and not *for* them.[19]

"If He Refuses to Listen Even to the Church…"

When all other attempts at restoration have failed and the brother still refuses to repent, it's time for the "radical surgery" of church discipline: withdrawal of fellowship by the whole church.[20]

Review No. 30 [1982], 39.

[19] As we will see in our study of Paul's texts on discipline, all of these "steps" are not required as a pattern for all cases (e.g., 1 Cor 5.1–8; Tit 3.10–11).

[20] France (2007, 693) is among those who maintain that "let him be to you" refers only to the original accuser and not to the church as a whole, because the Greek pronoun for "you" (*soi*) is singular and not plural. However, the earlier involvement of the church in the process and the switch to the second person plural in verse 18 show that this is

Jesus says to "let him be to you as a Gentile and a tax collector." Gentiles and tax collectors were categories of unclean people devout Jews avoided. Such avoidance not only expressed disapproval but also prevented the contamination of uncleanness from spreading among the people. Both concerns seem to be in view in verse 17 as Jesus speaks figuratively of the same principle among His followers: the sinning Christian must know that his behavior is unacceptable within the Christian fellowship, and the church must be put on the alert against imitating him. But even this drastic action of avoidance by the group as a whole has a positive intent: the hope that the sinning Christian will be grieved by the ostracism of his brothers and sisters and long to be included once again in the fellowship of believers.[21] But even if this doesn't happen, at least the church is preserved from his negative influence.[22]

"Whatever You Bind on Earth…"

While we often hear much about verses 15–17 in discussions of church discipline, we usually hear little, if anything, about verses 18–20. Yet they are an inherent part of the subject and add some important points, as important as the "procedural" discussion in the preceding verses.

---

to be a communal and not merely a personal act. See R.H. Gundry, *Matthew: A Commentary on His Literary and Theological Art* (Grand Rapids: Eerdmans, 1982), 368. If the end result were simply the avoidance of the offender by the original accuser, it would be difficult to understand the purpose of involving others in the process at all.

[21] Eugene Peterson offers this indefensible paraphrase of verse 17b: "If he won't listen to the church, you'll have to start from scratch, confront him with the need for repentance, and offer again God's forgiving love" (*The Message: The New Testament in Contemporary English* [Colorado Springs: NavPress, 1993], 46). The rationale for such a paraphrase is that Jesus loved and accepted tax collectors and Gentiles, so this is what is implied in His words in Matthew 18.17. However, this isn't what He *says* in this text, nor is it consistent with New Testament teaching elsewhere, as we shall see in our discussions of the Pauline texts. This can only be regarded as an unfortunate incidence of biased paraphrase replacing translation.

[22] On the entire subject of the expected results of such disciplinary action, see the discussion of 1 Corinthians 5 in Chapter Ten.

For one, verse 18 informs us that when the congregation unites in disciplinary action, it does so on behalf of God Himself, because we are thereby seeking to put into practice the teachings of His word. In addition, the church is assured that its actions are ratified by Heaven itself. This is not to suggest that the church can make up the rules as we go along but rather that "as the church is responsive to the guidance of God it will come to the decisions that have already been made in heaven."[23] The two agreeing in verse 19 is not, as we usually hear, about agreeing in prayer but about agreeing on the proper course of discipline. Likewise, the "two or three" gathered in Christ's name isn't a promise about our corporate worship, that God will be among us no matter how small the crowd (although that statement would certainly be true in that context), but a promise about our disciplinary decisions.[24] Jesus not only ratifies the solemn act of congregational discipline but participates with us in it, even as we do it. Perhaps it might help us in carrying out the difficult task of congregational discipline to remember that "Church discipline is not an action of merely human administration: it may count on the assistance and ratification of the risen Christ."[25] By His command we discipline, and with His help we carry out what He has commanded.[26]

---

[23] Leon Morris, *The Gospel According to Matthew* (Grand Rapids: Eerdmans, 1992), 469. R.T. France (1985, 275) adds that the church's refusal to overlook sin without rebuke carries with it the prior endorsement of heaven.

[24] According to J.D.M. Derrett, the phrase "where two or three are gathered together" has nothing to do with prayer. Rather, "It means that unofficial dispute settlers, peacemakers, perform a divine function" ("Where two or three are convened in my name…: a sad misunderstanding," *Expository Times* No. 91 [1979], 86).

[25] David Hill, *The Gospel of Matthew* (London: Oliphants, 1972), 276.

[26] This understanding of the church's role in discipline is quite different from that of Leeman, who says that discipline expresses the church's authority to determine who is and who is not actually a Christian. Since neither Jesus nor any other New Testament writer ever says this, it seems to be an exaggeration and misinterpretation of Matthew 18.19–20. See both his *Church Discipline* (35–45) and his longer work, *The Church and the Surprising Offense of God's Love: Reintroducing the Doctrines of Church Membership and*

Holiness and Fellowship?

But what, someone might ask, does all of this have to do with the themes of holiness, fellowship, and truth-telling which we identified earlier in our study as underlying all that the New Testament teaches about church discipline? By now this should be obvious. Holiness and truthfulness demand that we not be a people who ignore sin in our own lives or in our midst as a community of believers. They demand that when sin does occur, as it inevitably will, we must be willing to face up to it and attempt to rectify it, regardless of the difficulty. They even demand that, on occasion, we will separate ourselves from fellow believers whose lives are out of harmony with our Lord's teachings and who cannot be made to see that they are so or to change their behavior. Matthew 18.15–17 and indeed the entire eighteenth chapter of Matthew reminds us that we can only "share his holiness" (Heb 12.10) if we are willing to confront sin truthfully and remove it from our midst. But fellowship demands that we not do so too quickly or unlovingly, that we show the same care and concern for one weak, unattractive sheep that we would show for any other. It demands that we act as inconspicuously and discreetly as possible in order to preserve our brother's reputation and integrity. But it also demands that we act in concert as a body of believers to reclaim stubborn wanderers from the fold. And it reminds us that, as we do this in fellowship with one another, we are also doing so in fellowship with our Lord Himself.

Discipline (Wheaton, IL: Crossway, 2010), Chapter Four, for expressions of his views. In spite of this flawed understanding of the central role of discipline, Leeman has many excellent insights on the practicalities of carrying out discipline.

For Thought and Discussion

1. How does Matthew 18.15–17 show that sin should be taken seriously?

2. What criteria could you add for determining under what circumstances we should approach a sinning brother or sister for disciplinary purposes?

3. In what ways does Jesus remind us in Matthew 18.15–17 that the goal of discipline is to restore the sinner rather than to remove him/her from our fellowship?

4. Why is it important to keep discipline as private as possible but also to make it as public as necessary?

5. Have you ever personally gone to a brother or sister in the way Jesus describes in Matthew 18? What was the result of your efforts? What would you do differently if faced with the same situation again?

EIGHT

The Fine Art of Gentle Restoration

Galatians 6.1

So then be neither consenting to evil, so as to approve it; nor negligent so as not to reprove it; nor proud so as to reprove it in a tone of insult. (Augustine of Hippo)

For many years Irene had been an active member of her congregation. An accomplished teacher and zealous personal evangelist, she had been instrumental in leading numerous people to Christ and everyone in the church admired her. In every respect her life had been a model of Christian faithfulness and service. Then one day, word began to circulate around the small town where she lived that Irene had been accused of stealing money from her employer. She didn't deny the charges, and because she was a long-time employee, they were eventually dropped. But that wasn't all that was dropped. Irene moved on to another job and stopped attending church, although she remained in the community. Everyone in the congregation was stunned—so stunned, in fact, that no one said or did anything about the situation from a spiritual perspective. There were murmurings and whispered conservations, but no one approached Irene to discuss her sin. They were all too stunned; how could this happen to someone like Irene?

When a person whose faith we admire disappoints us in such a drastic way, it creates a kind of spiritual shock that is difficult to absorb. We're prone to think that surely this person was a hypocrite all along, that his or her profession of faith was false from the start, that "true Christians" simply can't commit such awful acts, and that anyone who would do such a thing is no longer worthy of our concern. We forget about the power of what Paul calls "the flesh," that tendency resident within all of us that causes us to act selfishly and pulls us away from God. According to Romans 8 and Galatians 5, the flesh is an ever-present danger whose power we dare not under-estimate. As the example of David, a "man after God's own heart," well testifies, even the best of God's servants is capable of shameful behavior. Our only hope is to trust in Christ and not in ourselves and to discipline ourselves to "walk by the Spirit" so that we won't "gratify the desires of the flesh."

But what happens when someone among us doesn't follow the Spirit's way, when they allow the flesh to have its way instead? What about someone like Irene? Can she be reclaimed, or must we simply write her off as a tragic loss? Do we have any responsibility to her, or has her behavior made her unworthy of our efforts?

The Spirit vs. the Flesh

It's clear from the opening of Paul's letter to the Galatians that he is writing to combat what he considers to be a drastic deviation from the gospel he had preached to them. In 1.6 he expresses astonishment that they had, within a relatively short period of time, abandoned his teaching and had embraced "a different gospel." He emphasizes that this isn't really another gospel but only a perversion of the one gospel and therefore not really "good news" at all (1.7). He then pronounces an "anathema" (a sentence of condemnation; see the additional note below) on anyone guilty of preaching a gospel contrary to his original message (1.8–9). Reading through the letter, the nature of the problem becomes clearer. It involved a conflict over justification, whether we are made right with God by works of the law or through faith in Christ (2.15–16). The seriousness of this issue becomes evident in 3.10 as Paul quotes Deuteronomy 27.26 to support his contention that "all who rely on works of the law are under a curse." Galatians 5.2 and 6.12 add the further nuance that the crux of the issue wasn't the law of Moses in its entirety, but circumcision, which had apparently become isolated as the epitome of law-keeping.[1]

The situation seems to be this: some unnamed persons (obviously Jewish Christians) were attempting to force the observance of the law on the Galatian Christians, who were mostly Gentiles. Apparently this demand was not presented in place of the gospel but in addition to it (5.2). Of particular concern to these "Judaizers,"[2] as they are usually called, was that the Galatians must submit to circumcision, since this was the sign of the covenant given to God's people Israel. If it took circumcision to be a Jew (one of God's people), they likely reasoned, why would it be any different for a Gentile wanting to become a Christian? In essence this meant that, in order to become a Christian, a Gentile would first need to become a Jew. Paul charges in 6.13 that this

---

[1] For background to this discussion, see Acts 15, where it is clear that some early Jewish Christians regarded circumcision as a "salvation issue," a viewpoint rejected by Paul and eventually by the majority of those present for what has come to be known as "The Jerusalem Council," which took place approximately AD 49. Although the issue of Gentile circumcision was resolved in theory at this meeting, it is clear from Paul's later references to it that not everyone bought into this decision (see Rom 2.28–29; 4.9–12; Phil 3.2–11; Col 2.8–15). It seems to me that Galatians was most likely written around AD 48, shortly before the conference in Jerusalem took place, since Paul does not cite its decision in combating the requirement of Gentile circumcision.

[2] This term is derived from a Greek verb meaning "to live like a Jew," which Paul uses in Galatians 2.14.

is the real issue and not the law as such and further alleges that these Jewish Christians were simply trying to escape persecution from their non-Christian Jewish neighbors, who would have disapproved of any Jew who associated with uncircumcised people (6.12). If the Gentiles would only accept circumcision, the tension between these Jewish believers and other Jews would be resolved. But Paul sees this as a serious breach of the basic principle of the gospel, that is, that justification comes only through faith in Christ, and he condemns it in no uncertain terms. He takes great paints to demonstrate conclusively that justification cannot possibly come through the law (2.21–4.31) and issues a stirring call to freedom: "For freedom Christ has set us free; stand firm therefore and do submit again to a yoke of slavery" (5.1). If the Galatians were to escape the slavery of law-keeping, they must insist on their freedom in Christ by refusing the demand for circumcision as an addition to the gospel.

But Freedom Is Never Free

Freedom always runs the risk of turning into libertinism, the attitude which says, "Because of Christ and God's grace, I can do anything I want." We know from Romans 3.8 and 6.1–2 that there were people in Paul's own day who were saying just that (or accusing Paul of teaching it; see also 1 Cor 10.23ff). So along with his call to freedom, Paul also issues a call to moral and ethical responsibility: "For you were called to freedom, brothers. Only do not use your freedom as an opportunity for the flesh, but through love serve one another" (5.13). From this point on through 6.10, he gives a series of instructions designed to combat the libertine attitude. He shows particular concern for the way Christians treat one another. In fact, his instructions about "walking by the Spirit" rather than "by the flesh" are framed with statements of a relational nature: "For the whole law is fulfilled in one word: 'You shall love your neighbor as yourself.' But if you bite and devour one another, watch out that you are not consumed by one another" (5.14–15). "Let us not become conceited, provoking one another, envying one another" (5.26). It may be that Paul knew of particular problems of this kind among the Galatians, or he may simply have been aware that libertinism inevitably results in the abuse of one's privileges at the expense of others. Either way, his instructions are pertinent.

It is in this context of warning the Galatians not to use their liberty as license that Paul admonishes them to exercise discipline. He has already urged upon them the necessity of "walking by the Spirit," which requires a spirit of humility and a concern for others' welfare. This concern must continue, he says, even when (perhaps *especially* when) a fellow Christian falls into sinful behavior.

> Brothers, even if a person is overtaken in some trespass, you who are spiritual restore such a one with a gentle spirit, looking out for yourselves, lest you also be tempted (Gal 6.1; my translation).

Notice the similarities between Paul's teaching and that of Jesus in Matthew 18.15–17 (see Chapters 6 and 7). In both texts the general concern is for Christian relationships. Both teach the necessity of a humble spirit toward one another. Both emphasize that even sin in someone's life does not make him or her unworthy of our love and attention, but rather calls for the concern of each individual and of the group as a whole in order to restore them to wholeness in their relationship with God and with the rest of the church.

Overtaken By Sin

As in the case of Jesus' instructions, Paul speaks of sin in a general way rather than of any specific situation or type of sin.

Any time a brother or sister[3] fails to "walk by the Spirit," there is a problem which requires attention from the larger group. There are two categories of church members in view here. One is "you who are spiritual," and the other is anyone who is "overtaken in some trespass."[4] We should not interpret "you who are spiritual" to mean some super-spiritual faction within the Galatian churches, such as evidently existed at Corinth (1 Cor 4.6–14; such hyper-spiritual factionalism is also suggested by the entire discussion of spiritual gifts in 1 Cor 12–14). The context requires us to understand "you who are spiritual" simply as those who *are* walking by the Spirit as Paul directed in 5.16–26. So "the spiritual" are the church as a whole who are consistently practicing Christian principles in their lives.[5] The other category of church member is the one who will on occasion deviate seriously from Christian practices, who is not "walking by the Spirit"—someone like Irene. This person Paul describes as having been "overtaken in some trespass."

The word translated "overtaken" (*prolambano*) may suggest either that the person has been inadvertently involved in wrong-doing or that he/she has been "surprised" or "detected" in sin by another Christian.[6] In neither case is the trespass excusable, although the former sense might indicate that the individual did not deliberately set out to do what he ended up doing. But regard-

---

[3] The Revised Standard Version has "a man," but the Greek word *anthropos* is more correctly translated "person." The ESV translates it more properly as "anyone"; likewise, the New International Version has "someone."

[4] The Greek noun *paraptoma* seems to be used in a generic sense of "sin" rather than of any specific type of sin.

[5] Frank J. Matera, *Galatians* (Collegeville, Minnesota: The Liturgical Press, 1992) says *hymeis* (plural "you") "refers to all of the Galatians, not to a special group" (213). Likewise, Martinus C. de Boer, *Galatians: A Commentary* (Louisville, Kentucky: Westminster John Knox Press, 2011): "You who are spiritual" is "an inclusive description, coined by Paul himself, of the 'brethren'" who are addressed in 1.2, 11; 3.15; 4.12, 28, 31; 5.11, 13.

[6] This explains the ESV translation: "caught in any transgression."

less of the precise intention of Paul's verb, his overall meaning is clear: the one who falls into sin cannot simply be ignored by the rest. Such people are certainly not beyond hope, regardless of the shocking nature of their sin. And their sin must be recognized and dealt with appropriately.

"Restore Such a One"

Specifically, what action should "the spiritual" take on behalf of the one overtaken in sin? We might expect to find at this point a repetition of Jesus' words from Matthew 18, the "steps" toward regaining a sinner. In fact, as we will see later, Paul never quotes the words of Jesus from Matthew 18 precisely, as if he regarded them as some sort of legal formula which must be followed to the letter in every case.

In Galatians 6.1 the required action is summed up in the single verb "restore," which is Paul's term for bringing back the erring Christian to the Spirit's way. The verb *katartizo* occurs in Matthew 4.21 and Mark 1.19 for the mending of fish nets, in 1 Corinthians 1.10 as a term for Christian unity, and in 2 Corinthians 13.11 as an appeal to "mend your ways." It has the connotation of restoring someone or something to proper order. And isn't the goal of discipline as we have seen so far to restore someone to a life of walking by the Spirit rather than by the flesh, to restore him to fellowship with God and with God's people, and to restore fractured relationships within the church when they have been disrupted by sin?

While Paul says nothing about the *process* of restoration, he focuses on the ultimate *goal* of that process—in Jesus' words, "regaining your brother." Again we are reminded of the real purpose of discipline, not to punish or eliminate or control but to restore. And we can readily see how Jesus' more specific teachings fit under the umbrella of Paul's verb "to restore." Going to a sinning

Christian privately, involving others in our efforts to persuade, telling it to the church—even complete avoidance—are all aimed at the restoration of broken lives and broken relationships.

"With a Gentle Spirit"

If we are to do this kind of restoration effectively, we must go about it in a specific manner: "with a gentle spirit." Those who are walking by the Spirit must not assume an attitude of spiritual superiority to those overtaken in sin, as though it "could never happen to me." It isn't a case of "the righteous" pointing the accusing finger at "the sinful" (another reason, I think, to prefer the translation "overtaken" rather than "caught"). The spiritual are to go with a deep sense of gentle humility to those who were once spiritual like themselves yet who have fallen into "fleshly" ways. In fact, Paul goes on to caution the spiritual to "look out for themselves,"[7] for fear they might fall into the same sort of sin. We are never in a proper frame of mind to deal with other people's sins until we are deeply conscious of our own weaknesses and failings. Only then can we have the necessary spirit of humility and gentleness. In this way—and in this spirit—we can truly "bear one another's burdens" (6.2).

Restoration, Anyone?

What does all of this say about our failures to restore one another when necessary? Surely we have to admit that not much of this goes on in today's church. Most of the time we are content if people such as Irene simply go away and spare the church further embarrassment. What does our failure imply? Obviously it suggests we are not taking sin as seriously as did Jesus and Paul. We are prone

---

[7] Paul uses a participle to express the ongoing necessity of such a humble approach: "looking out for yourselves," as in my translation above. See also the ESV's "Keep watch on yourselves," which is preferable to RSV's "Look to yourself."

to act only if forced by circumstances (such as abject embarrassment to the church). As long as the surface of the waters appears untroubled, we are generally content to ignore the dangerous currents beneath. Another implication is that we fail to acknowledge the distinction between those who walk by the Spirit and those who don't. Paul says "the works of the flesh are *evident*" (ESV, 5.19), but we sometimes act as if no one can possibly discern who is sinning and who isn't. Still another implication is the implicit denial of our fellowship, that we are, in fact, spiritually bound together and obligated to one another. "Brother" and "sister" are not just titles; they suggest relationships, and relationship implies responsibility, our responsibility to act when a fellow-Christian is in trouble.

There's really no question what the church should have done when Irene left the Spirit's way; her brothers and sisters should have sought to restore her with a gentle spirit, and perhaps they might have been successful had they tried. Such sin in the life of a Christian is a terrible thing, but it isn't necessarily fatal. People do actually repent, and when they do, God forgives them. It may well be that our loving confrontation, gently and humbly stated, will be all it takes to bring someone like Irene back to the Lord and to His people. How can we not act on that possibility?

Additional Note:
Does Galatians 1.8–9 Relate to Early Christian Discipline?

In the world of New Testament scholarship, there is a rather ironic reversal that often takes place in regard to Galatians and its teaching about church discipline. On the one hand, many scholars fail to recognize the disciplinary nature of Galatians 6.1, while at the same time trying to say that Galatians 1.8–9 concerns early Christian discipline. The problem lies in the frequently-made assumption that the early church employed curses against offenders in their midst which resulted in (or were expected to result in) their physical deaths. Advocates of this concept find support in such texts as Acts 5.1–11 (the punitive deaths of Ananias and Sapphira) and 1 Corinthians 11.29–30 (failure to "discern the body" at the Lord's Supper, resulting in illness and death).[8]

Following this line of reasoning, some scholars interpret Galatians 1.8–9 as a typical text on early church discipline. Paul pronounces the "anathema"[9] on those who preach another gospel, supposedly expecting them to die physically as a result. In his highly influential commentary on Galatians, Hans Dieter Betz describes Galatians 1.8–9 as "an instance of early church discipline" and "the first instance of Christian excommunication,"[10] based on the occurrence of *anathema* in some ancient Greek magical texts. As a result of Betz's claims, many others have followed him in coming to this conclusion.[11]

First, we should note that Paul's use of *anathema* is based not on Greek magical texts, but on the Septuagint (the Old Testament in Greek), where it appears frequently. In the Old Testament *anathema* designates that which is "devoted to the Lord for destruction" (as in Josh 6.17; Num 21.3; Ez 10.8). The point of Paul's use of the term is to proclaim the law of God which is operative under certain conditions; that is, if anyone preaches a different gospel than what Paul preached, he automatically falls under God's curse, not the church's or Paul's curse. He does not intend by use of a curse to bring about the sentence of condemnation; he merely announces the way things are.

Second, the following points should be observed concerning the claim that Galatians 1.8–9 is a text on church discipline:

---

[8] Further discussion of this point of view will accompany our study of 1 Corinthians 5 (see Chapter 10), since "deliver ... to Satan" in that chapter is also interpreted as the employment of a curse leading to death.

[9] "Anathema" is the transliteration into English of the Greek word *anathema*, which the ESV translates as "let him be accursed."

[10] *Galatians: A Commentary on Paul's Letter to the Churches in Galatia* (Philadelphia: Fortress, 1970), 54. See the detailed critique of Betz's interpretation in my *Disciplinary Practices in Pauline Texts*, 117–28.

[11] See Calvin J. Roetzel, *Judgment in the Community* (Leiden: E.J. Brill, 1972), 120–21 for a pertinent example. However, it is noteworthy that most recent commentators on Galatians do not even entertain this possibility.

(1) There is no evidence that *anathema* was ever used in a disciplinary sense in the First Century. It was used in this way in later centuries, primarily by Roman Catholics, but not until long after Paul's time. (See, for example, Rom 9.3 and 1 Cor 12.3, where this sense is obviously excluded.)

(2) Paul's statement in Galatians 1.8–9 does not call for any corporate act on the part of the church and therefore cannot be construed as church discipline.

(3) The pagan texts which supposedly serve as models for a disciplinary understanding of Galatians 1.8–9 are not disciplinary in nature since their goal isn't restoration to spiritual wholeness or to Christian fellowship. "They were apparently simply pronounced by angry people who wished evil and misery upon some luckless enemy."[12]

(4) There is no supporting evidence that Paul or any of the churches under his influence used curses in the exercise of church discipline. Scholars base this assumption solely on a skewed interpretation of Galatians 1.8–9.[13]

The curse/death interpretation of church discipline must be rejected as a serious distortion of what early Christian discipline was all about. Instead, we must look to texts such as Galatians 6.1, which carry forward the teaching of Jesus concerning loving care for each individual member of the church, even those "overtaken in some trespass."

For Thought and Discussion

1. State in your own words what Paul means by "flesh" and "spirit" in Galatians 5.16 and 6.1.

2. Why do you think Paul does not specify the kinds of sin which need attention in Galatians 6.1?

---

[12] J.E. Mignard, "Jewish and Christian Cultic Discipline to the Middle of the Second Century (Unpublished Ph.D. dissertation, Boston University, 1966), 38.

[13] Many of the same points apply to the discussion of 1 Corinthians 16.22, which is also subjected by many to the same curse/death interpretation as Galatians 1.8–9. See South, *Disciplinary Practices in Pauline Texts*, 133–36.

3. Who are "the spiritual" in Galatians 6.1? How can you tell?

4. What might be the hazards of failing to "look out for yourselves" in the exercise of church discipline? Do you know of instances where this was not done? What was the outcome?

5. How does the curse/death interpretation of Galatians 1.8–9 (and of 1 Cor 5.1–8) contradict the teachings of Jesus concerning church discipline?

NINE

Disciplining the Disorderly
2 Thessalonians 3.6–15

An important and sometimes neglected part of evangelism is to win Christians to Christianity, to disciple disciples, to win the *church* to Christ. (F.D. Bruner, *Matthew*)

John and Emily were intelligent, college-educated Christians with a lively family of six young children. In spite of their rather heavy family obligations, they tended to be a bit "quirky." John was an aspiring author and preferred not to be burdened with an ordinary job so he could be free to be creative and look for his big break. He would accept employment only temporarily and when forced to do so by necessity. Since Emily was totally occupied with the children and their numerous health problems and therefore unable to work, economic hardship was a way of life. Time and again John and Emily approached the leaders of their church for help and usually received what they requested. Although the elders and benevolence committee were somewhat put off by John's refusal to work steadily, the decision was usually made on the basis of the children; after all, it wasn't their fault that their parents were unwilling to put forth more effort to provide for them. So over a period of years the amount of help extended into multiple thousands of dollars. This continued until John one day deserted his family and disappeared and Emily pulled away from the church, whose leaders finally concluded that their obligation to this difficult family had run its course.

Similar stories have been repeated in churches more often than we care to admit. What do we do about people whose life-style isn't exactly respectable but who aren't committing any of the "serious" sins such as theft or adultery? And how far do we go in our compassion when such a situation continues and never seems to get any better, when it seems that the people involved could do something to make their situation better but simply choose not to? Do the Scriptures offer us any help, and is there any type of disciplinary action which might prove useful in not only ending a frustrating and wasteful situation for the church but also in getting people more in line with God's will for their lives and perhaps saving them from even worse deviations?

"The Disorderly" at Thessalonica

A careful reading of 2 Thessalonians 3:6–15 reveals that such frustrating situations as John and Emily's are nothing new. The young church at Thessalonica, too, had a problem with members whose lives were out of line. In what amounts to a major section of this brief letter, Paul gives some rather explicit instructions regarding them:

> But we command you, brothers, in the name of the Lord Jesus Christ, to hold yourselves aloof from every brother who conducts himself in a disorderly manner and not in keeping with the tradition which you received from us. For you yourselves know the necessity of imitating us, because we were not disorderly among you, nor did we eat bread from anyone without paying, but with toil and hardship we worked night and day in order not to burden

any of you. Not that we do not have the right, but in order to give you in us an example to imitate. For when we were with you, we commanded you this: If anyone does not wish to work, then do not let him eat. For we hear that some among you are conducting themselves in a disorderly manner, not busy but busybodies. Now we command and exhort such people in the Lord Jesus Christ to work quietly and eat their own bread. But the rest of you, brothers, do not become weary in the good you are doing. If anyone does not obey what we say by means of this letter, take notice of that person and do not associate with him, so that he will be put to shame. Do not regard him as an enemy, but admonish him as a brother. (my translation)

Comparing my translation above with some of the more common ones (NIV, RSV, NRSV, ESV), you notice right away a major difference: while most translations interpret the problem at Thessalonica as Christians "living (or "walking," ESV) in idleness," I have chosen to stay with the more literal rendering, "conducting themselves in a disorderly manner." Scholars and commentaries are about evenly divided over whether to translate it in the more specific or more general fashion. Some argue that the context demands that "living in idleness" is the correct translation. They would even go so far as to translate 1 Thessalonians 5.14 as "Admonish the idle" (ESV), even though nothing in the immediate context of 1 Thessalonians 5 requires it.[1]

I have chosen the more literal and more general translation because the basic meaning of *ataktos* is not "idle" but "disorderly" or "undisciplined." Ancient writers used it to describe the disorderliness of matter prior to creation, of soldiers who were out of rank or shirking their duties, and even of irregular worship services.[2] I

---

[1] The translation of 1 Thessalonians 5.14 in this way seems to be an inference drawn from 2 Thessalonians 3.

[2] For the specific ancient references, see South, *Disciplinary Practices in Pauline Texts*,

don't question that at least part of the specific problem at Thessalonica was people "living in idleness," but translating *ataktos* in this way may obscure the reality that there was more at issue than mere idleness and that idleness was only one manifestation of a larger problem. The larger problem seems to have been the authority of the apostle Paul himself. The disorderliness of some Thessalonian Christians lay in the fact that they were not living "in keeping with the tradition which you received from us" and in keeping with the example set by the apostle and his associates while working among the believers there. This tradition apparently included instructions about Christian living as well as doctrine and was backed up by the personal example of Paul and his friends. So in trying to correct the situation, he "commands" and "exhorts" in the name of Jesus (vv 6 and 12) and reminds them of an earlier command which they had been given but which they had not obeyed. Likewise, Paul made it clear in verse 14 that further refusal to obey "what we say in this letter" was to be regarded as a serious offense. So the misconduct of the *ataktoi* ("disorderly ones") was a matter not only of not working but of disregard for Paul's apostolic authority. Furthermore, verse 11 shows that not working was not the only manifestation of disorderliness among the Thessalonians. Some were "not busy but busybodies" (to preserve the word-play in Greek). They not only needed to work, but to "work quietly" (mind their own business).

The traditional understanding of the idleness at Thessalonica is that it was the result of the mistaken belief that Jesus was to return soon; thus the normal routines of life—including working for a living—were meaningless. This is a plausible reconstruction of the situation, since both Thessalonian letters indicate that misunderstandings of the coming of Jesus were part of the problem at Thessalonica. However, nothing in either letter connects these

162.

misunderstandings with the problem of idleness. It may be that the two problems were unrelated, since even today many refuse to work who have no particular convictions about the coming of the Lord. The disorderly people at Thessalonica may simply have liked the idea of others providing for them, as did John and Emily. [3]

The Power of Brotherly Avoidance

So how should the church as a whole respond to such disorderly members? Paul commands two concurrent courses of action: avoidance and continued warning. The command to avoid the disorderly comes in verses 6 and 14, where two rather general terms are used: "hold yourselves aloof from" (*stello*) and "do not associate with" (*me sunanamignymi*). The first word is a term of general avoidance or withdrawal. The second means literally "not to be mingled with." These aren't very specific instructions, so we must ask further exactly what Paul had in mind. The other commanded course of action, continued warning, helps interpret the first. Whatever might have been involved in "avoiding" the disorderly, it obviously stopped short of expelling them from the church's fellowship entirely, since it was assumed there would be sufficient contact for warnings and admonitions to occur. Perhaps Paul had in mind generally avoiding the disorderly in social settings but continuing to associate with them at worship or other church activities. Verse 10 implies that the disorderly were to remain within the community of believers but were to be denied some of the privileges of membership, specifically the right to sit at the common table where believers shared their food. [4] Regardless of the

---

[3] For a series of persuasive arguments against the traditional understanding of the Thessalonian idleness, see B.N. Kaye, "Eschatology and Ethics in 1 and 2 Thessalonians," *Novum Testamentum* 17 (1975), 47–57.

[4] Although some see v 10 as a reference to the Lord's Supper, it seems probable that Paul's reference is more general. The connection between not working and not eating argues for a more mundane understanding of "eating." Plus, refusing someone the right

specific actions involved, "Do not let him eat" must have surely excluded providing material support for disorderly members, particularly those who refused to work to support themselves.

This brings up two important points. First, we have in this verse a specific example of what was said in an earlier chapter about discipline and its necessary context, a close-knit Christian fellowship. Verses 10 raises many interesting questions about early Christian table fellowship, but one thing seems clear: the fellowship and mutual dependence were close enough that the larger body could deprive the disorderly of the right to eat. Does this help us understand why our disciplinary efforts are frequently so ineffective? Isn't it simply a reflection of our puny fellowship? As I. H. Marshall has well put it, "One may suspect … that the nature of the Christian community has changed. Discipline is possible and necessary within a fairly compact, closely-related group, but this may not be so in the rather loose association typical of many modern congregations."[5] Are today's churches anything like the close-knit and mutually-dependent Thessalonian church, or are we merely a "rather loose association" of people who happen to meet for worship in the same location? The answer will tell us much about our ability (or inability) to discipline effectively. This may seem like an argument against the possibility of discipline in today's churches, since there is seldom this kind of material/financial dependence. But such interdependence does occur, as in John and Emily's case, and it reinforces the earlier point that before we can strengthen our discipline, we must strengthen our fellowship. This becomes especially important in larger churches, which will

---

to eat the communion would seem to involve a more complete exclusion from the community of believers, which Paul doesn't seem to have in mind here.

[5] *1 and 2 Thessalonians* (Grand Rapids: Eerdmans, 1983), 229. This should not be taken to mean, however, that simply because churches today are larger we are relieved of the responsibility to practice discipline.

likely need to work even harder to have the kind of fellowship and accountability that comes more readily in smaller groups.

The other significant point to observe is that verse 10 concerns discipline *within the congregation* and does not give instructions for conducting the church's "benevolence" ministry. When genuinely needy people come to the church for help, we ought not to apply verse 10 indiscriminately. Some are unable to help themselves, and to require that they rake leaves or wash windows before we will help them can be cruel. Our help may come in the form of a job for those who are able to perform one, but 2 Thessalonians 3.10 ought not to be our primary rule of thumb for dealing with people in need. On the other hand, we probably should employ it more often than we do in the case of Christians such as John and Emily, who habitually rely on the church to do for them what they could do for themselves. Ironically, we are sometimes more "benevolent" toward people who need discipline than toward those who need benevolence. Although 2 Thessalonians 3.6–15 does not deal exclusively with idleness but rather with "disorderliness" in general, it certainly provides us with practical guidance in dealing with "John and Emily" situations.

"Warn Him as a Brother"

As in all the texts we have examined so far, Paul's concern for the Thessalonians was not only the health and purity of the church but also the salvation of individual Christians, even the erring ones. He continues to refer to such an offender as a "brother" (vv 6 and 15) and cautions the Thessalonians not to "regard him as an enemy" but to "admonish him as a brother." He still belongs to Christ, and, although his life is out of harmony with Christ's will, the situation does not call for more drastic action, such as treating him "as a Gentile or a tax collector."[6]

---

[6] The Stoic philosopher and emperor Marcus Aurelius likewise advises the avoidance

This raises an important question: Why doesn't Paul speak more specifically about what he wants the church to do in regard to the disorderly? Why does he employ the general terms of avoidance and warning rather than give more specific instructions such as those found in Matthew 18.15–17 and 1 Corinthians 5.5? The answer may be that "it is difficult, if not impossible, to frame precise rules when dealing with personal relationships."[7] Even in situations requiring discipline, people are still people, and hard-and-fast rules are seldom helpful. It would seem that Paul has deliberately left his instructions ambiguous within the broad outlines of avoidance and brotherly admonition. The point is to achieve the desired results of maintaining the church's health and holiness as well as encouraging the offender's salvation. Paul leaves it open to the church to decide exactly what might be required in the case at hand in order to accomplish these goals. It is important to note that Paul does not here, as in Galatians 6.1, repeat the steps outlined in Matthew 18.15–17, although he could have done so easily enough. Instead he leaves the church free to take whatever action might be necessary to reclaim the particular offender and to protect the church at large. If a relatively informal course of warning and admonition accomplishes the purpose, there is no need to go further, since the goal is restoration, not punishment. More stringent warnings and more complete avoidance may be brought to bear if lesser measures fail. Paul does not command the specific steps to be taken; what he does command is that the church do what it can to remedy the situation.

---

of those who behave roughly and rudely, and like Paul, says not to treat them as enemies. However, he gives no counsel concerning reforming such people. "The Stoic individualism and the Christian sense of obligation towards a brother are thrown into sharp contrast... " (James Moffatt, "2 Thessalonians iii.14, 15," *Expository Times* 21 [1909–10], 328).

[7] Marshall, 228.

Practically speaking, what options are open to a congregation in dealing with disorderly members? What exactly does brotherly avoidance coupled with continued warning look like, and how does it work? What specifically might a church do in order to correct the disorderly short of a total withdrawal of fellowship? The possibilities are as varied as the situations which might prompt them. One might be, as suggested above, continued association in worship but limited association at a social level. However, since in all congregations there are members who have little or no outside association with other believers, the purposes of such limitations would have to be made explicit—that is, that the person is being avoided for a specific reason and for redemptive purposes. Paul reinforces this necessity by speaking to the entire Thessalonian church about such action rather than to only a few, certainly not only to the elders or other leaders. In such a situation, all encounters, whether at worship or in other settings, could become occasions for warning and admonition. The point would be not to allow the disorderly brother or sister the enjoyment of Christian fellowship without the mutual responsibilities required by genuine fellowship. If every encounter with fellow believers resulted in admonitions and warnings, the disorderly would soon be forced to decide how important their fellowship is to them and whether or not they want it to continue. This more than adequately explains Paul's reference to shame in verse 14.

In cases such as John and Emily's—where the disorderliness involves an over-dependence on the church for some type of support, whether material or emotional—Paul's words are immediately relevant. The refusal to correct misbehavior should result in having that support cut off. An example of non-material support would be someone who continually seeks counseling from church leaders but refuses to accept their guidance in matters of spiritual discipline. Such people can become a constant drain on the time and emotional energy of church leaders, and if they refuse to do what they can to help themselves, the situation should not be allowed to continue. If this type of action seems harsh or unloving, we should ask ourselves what those Thessalonians thought who showed up at the fellowship meal or the church pantry only to be denied access, or who found themselves admonished each time they arrived for worship. Just as in raising a child, there are times when the truly loving course of action is to allow the disorderly to experience the consequences of their chosen path. Failure to do so would be decidedly unloving since it reinforces sinful behavior which could result in the loss of their relationship with God altogether, to say nothing of the damage done to the church. In circumstances where such action seems called for, we must trust the wisdom of God that it will be more effective in redeeming the disorderly than a softer approach which may on the surface seem more loving but which actually may be motivated by the fact that it is easier for us. No one ever said that discipline would or should be easy.

The important fact to note at this point is that church discipline cannot be reduced to a sequence of steps to be applied in all cases. This isn't what Paul did, and churches in our own time often make discipline more difficult and less effective by not recognizing the built-in flexibility of the divine instructions. In dealing with erring members there is a wide range of options, within the broad guidelines found in this text and others, and we should be ready to use them all, if necessary, to reclaim one of Christ's lost sheep or to caution one just beginning to stray. We can go astray in many ways. Praise God that He provides numerous means for returning us to His fold!

For Thought and Discussion

1. Have you known of "John and Emily" situations in churches where you have worshiped? How were these situations handled? What was the eventual outcome? Do you think discipline could have made a difference? Why or why not?

2. Why do you think churches are usually so slow to apply disciplinary principles in "John and Emily" situations?

3. What are some specific ways in which Christians might practice avoidance in dealing with fellow-believers who are disorderly in the ways Paul describes? In what other ways might someone lead a "disorderly" life that would require intervention by other Christians?

4. In what ways do Paul's instructions to the Thessalonians presume a close-knit fellowship of believers? What might be the results if a church lacking in close fellowship attempted to do what Paul says in 1 Thessalonians 3.6–15?

5. What should we conclude from the fact that Paul gives rather general instructions about how to treat disorderly members? How does this compare to the ways you have seen discipline practiced?

TEN

Extreme Discipline: Incest at Corinth

1 Corinthians 5.1–8

Cheap grace is the preaching of forgiveness without requiring repentance, baptism without church discipline, Communion without confession, absolution without personal confession. (Dietrich Bonhoeffer, *The Cost of Discipleship*)

First Corinthians 5.1–8 is one of the few New Testament texts on discipline which deal not only with a specific sin but with a specific *case* of sin, so it is therefore of particular interest in any study of church discipline. But because it does deal with a specific case, and a drastic one at that, we must keep in mind that it does not constitute a pattern for all instances of church discipline. Rather, it supplies guidance for dealing with extreme cases of moral deviation among Christians, and its voice should be heard more often than it normally is. The texts discussed so far deal with sin in a more general sense, and it is from them that we should draw our basic principles of action, such as concern for the salvation of the offender, dealing with sin as privately as possible, attempting to restore those who are overtaken in sin, and handling each situation individually and not according to some hard-and-fast scheme of disciplinary steps. In other words, it's important that we realize not every case of discipline should involve delivering someone to Satan.

A Shocking Situation

The problem Paul addressed in 1 Corinthians 5.1–8 was a drastic one indeed, because it had far-reaching consequences not only for the man committing the sin but also for the entire congregation. As a reading of both of Paul's extant letters to Corinth[1] shows, his relationship with this church was a stormy one, to say the least. Not only was the church allowing itself to be overly influenced by the pagan culture around it, there were also numerous challenges to Paul's authority as an apostle of Christ. This was especially the case when he spoke authoritatively in dealing with some of the errant behavior and theology that seems to have permeated the church. Rather than retreating, however, Paul spoke straightforwardly about the problems at hand, at least partly to test their willingness to be obedient (2 Cor 2.9). His instructions regarding a particularly shocking case of sexual immorality are very direct:

> Sexual immorality is actually reported among you, even such immorality as is not (permitted) among pagans, to the extent that someone has his father's wife. And you are puffed up! Should you not have mourned instead, so that the one who has done this deed might be removed from your midst? For I, being absent in body but present in spirit, have already, as one who is present, judged the one who has done this. When you are assembled

---

[1] Keep in mind that Paul apparently wrote two additional letters to this church that have not survived, which are mentioned in 1 Corinthians 5.9 (the "Previous Letter") and 2 Corinthians 2.1–4 and 7.8–12 (the "Sorrowful Letter"). The fact that these letters did not survive may itself bear testimony to the conflicts between Paul and the Corinthians, since they were apparently quite critical of the behavior of some within the congregation.

in the name of the Lord Jesus and my spirit (is there) with the power of our Lord Jesus, deliver that man to Satan for the destruction of the flesh, in order that the spirit may be saved in the day of the Lord. Your boasting is not good. Do you not know that just a small amount of leaven ferments the entire lump of dough? Remove the old leaven so that you may be new dough, just as you are unleavened. For our Passover lamb, Christ, has been sacrificed. To this end let us celebrate the feast, not with the old leaven which is the leaven of malice and evil, but with the unleavened bread of sincerity and truth. (my translation)

Although some specific aspects of the situation at Corinth remain unknown, its general outline is clear. Someone in the church is involved in an ongoing[2] sexual liaison with "his father's wife." The unusual expression "his father's wife" virtually assures that the woman involved is not the offender's mother, since that would have been easy enough for Paul to have said—and there seems little question that he would have done so had that been the case. Also, the expression "his father's wife" occurs in Leviticus 20.11, Deuteronomy 23.1, and Deuteronomy 27.20 to refer to a stepmother. It is unclear whether the man's father is still living or if he is divorced from his wife. Since Paul shows no particular concern for the woman's conduct or states how the church should respond to her, it seems safe to assume that she is not a Christian.

It isn't surprising that a case of sexual immorality might occur in a Christian congregation. After all, immorality was a prominent feature of the pagan moral landscape in which churches such as Corinth existed, as attested by Paul's frequent warnings against it (Gal 5.18–21; Eph 5.3–5; Col 3.5–10; etc.). But the case of immorality at Corinth is particularly shocking because it is "such as is not (permitted) among pagans." In my translation I

---

[2] The present infinitive (*echein*) indicates that this was not a one-time offense but a continuing one.

have placed the word "permitted" in parentheses because there is no corresponding verb in Greek. Paul literally says, "such immorality as is not among pagans." However, he surely doesn't mean that such cases never *occurred* among pagans,[3] but rather that such behavior was neither lawful nor acceptable. In fact such liaisons were forbidden by Roman law and were looked upon with revulsion in Greek and Roman society alike. But the condemnations and allegations found in ancient sources prove that such practices did exist in pagan society.[4] But even there they did not exist with approval, and Paul is alarmed that such is being tolerated in the church of Christ.[5]

Not only is the presence of immorality offensive to Paul, but so is the church's attitude toward it: "And you are puffed up!"[6] Why would a church be arrogant about having such sin occurring among its members? Apparently there was an air of broadmindedness prevailing at Corinth that could not be offended by even so repugnant a situation as this. It may well be that the

---

[3] However, this seems to be the import of many standard translations: "and such fornication as is not so much as named among the Gentiles" (KJV); "and of a kind that is not found even among pagans" (RSV, NRSV); "and of a kind that does not occur even among pagans" (NIV); "and immorality of such a kind as does not exist even among the Gentiles" (NASB). Such translations are justifiable only if Paul is understood as saying that such immorality does not exist *with approval* from Gentile society, since it is beyond question that such things did "occur." It seems more accurate to supply a more realistic verb, such as "permitted."

[4] For examples from various Greek and Roman sources, see South, *Disciplinary Practices in Pauline Texts*, 29–30.

[5] Based on such evidence, the translation offered by Raymond F. Collins is inexplicable: "such as does not exist among the Gentiles" (*First Corinthians* [Collegeville, MN: Liturgical Press, 1999], 2–5). David Garland is more on the mark when he translates, "the sort of sexual immorality not even tolerated among the Gentiles" (*1 Corinthians* [Grand Rapids: Baker Academic, 2003], 155. However, two pages later Garland paraphrases Paul's words as, "this kind of *porneia* is not even heard of (no verb is expressed in the Greek text) among them" (Garland, 157).

[6] "Puffed up" (*physioo*) is an expression which occurs often in this letter as an indication of the arrogance which infected the Corinthian church. Note the allegations of arrogance in chapters 1–4, 8, and 13.

Corinthians felt their superior spirituality (4.8) was vast enough to tolerate such things, and they were proud of that fact, if not of the situation itself.[7]

It isn't unusual in our own time to see churches overreact to legalism and a judgmental spirit by becoming overly tolerant and even proud of their superior understanding, a quality not possessed by their less enlightened brothers. The situation at Corinth should be sufficient warning of the danger of such an attitude. Here was a church that should have been in mourning over the wickedness in their midst and their failure to deal with it in a godly way, but pride had overruled repentance. No wonder Paul was dismayed![8]

Somebody Do Something!

Paul unhesitatingly calls for the most drastic disciplinary measures outlined anywhere in the New Testament. His goal is not only to deal with the incestuous man's sin, but also to correct the church's arrogant spirit.

First Paul says that the one who has done such a thing must be "removed from your midst" (v 2), and then outlines the prescribed action more specifically in verses 3–5. Paul's reaction to this immoral situation is in sharp contrast to that of the Corinthians, as brought out by the Greek construction of verse 3, where "For I…" stands at the beginning of the sentence in contrast to "And you…" at the beginning of verse 2. The Corinthi-

---

[7] Garland says, however, "It is more likely that Paul speaks of their boasting despite the immorality rather than because of it (4.6, 18, 19)". He notes that this is a change of mind from an earlier publication of his, and he offers persuasive arguments for his current view. See also Roy E. Ciampa and Brian S. Rosner, *The First Letter to the Corinthians* (Grand Rapids/Cambridge, U.K.: William B. Eerdmans Publishing Company, 2010), 202, who concur with Garland's revised view on the cause of the Corinthians' boasting.

[8] Garland points out that, "Since Paul directs all of his commands to the church body, we can infer that he is more vexed with the congregation than he is with the culprit" (153). See also Ciampa and Rosner, who point out that the second person plural occurs nine times in chapter 5 (206).

ans' arrogance may be preventing them from correcting this situation, but Paul will not be deterred by their spiritual indolence and tells them specifically what must be done. Although not physically present, Paul is present "in spirit,"[9] and has already judged the situation just as if he were there.[10] There is no question in Paul's mind what the church must do: meeting in solemn assembly, they are to "deliver that man to Satan" (v 5).

But what does Paul intend by this strange command? Not surprisingly, it has been the subject of much speculation and debate. The expression "to deliver to Satan" is unusual and occurs elsewhere in the New Testament only in 1 Timothy 1.20, where Paul refers to Hymenaeus and Alexander, "whom I have handed over to Satan that they may learn not to blaspheme."[11] The verb *paradounai* means "to deliver" or "hand over" and suggests that Paul intends the offender to be given over in some sense to the power of Satan. He doesn't pause to elaborate but moves on to express the intended result of this "handing over": "for the destruction of the flesh that the spirit[12] may be saved in the day of the Lord." In spite of the many scholars who claim that what Paul has in mind is the use of a

[9] It is difficult to know exactly what Paul means by his "spiritual presence" as stated in verses 3 and 4. He certainly implies more than just, "I'll be thinking about you," and seems somehow to see himself as "with them" spiritually. Certainly the letter itself conveyed a sense of Paul's presence as an apostle of Christ as it was read in the assembly. See 2 Corinthians 10.10–11, where Paul emphasizes that the dichotomy between his bodily presence and his "letter presence," at least as it was viewed by his opponents, is a false one.

[10] Notice that while many take Jesus' teaching against judging ("Judge not, that you be not judged." Matt 7.1) as a blanket condemnation of any kind of moral or ethical discrimination, Paul certainly did not interpret it that way. See also 1 Corinthians 5.12–13. Likewise, any realistic reading of the wider teachings of Jesus will show that His intent was not to forbid ever saying that someone else's conduct is wrong. See, for example, Matthew 7.6 and, again, 18.15–18.

[11] This is the ESV rendering of 1 Timothy 1.20, which for some reason translates the same phrase as both "deliver to Satan" (1 Cor 5.5) and "handed over to Satan" (1 Tim 1.20).

[12] Unlike almost all English translations of this verse, there is no word for "his" in the Greek, but this is the obvious intention.

curse ("deliver to Satan") expected to result in death ("the destruction of the flesh"), the context makes it clear that Paul is talking about putting him out of the church, what is often described as "disfellowshipping," "shunning," or "excommunication."[13]

The following observations support this conclusion:

(1) Paul has already said that the incestuous man should be "removed from your midst" (v 2).[14]

(2) In verses 6–8 Paul draws heavily on the Passover theme, particularly with reference to the Feast of Unleavened Bread which occurred just prior to Passover, during which the Israelites were to remove all "old leaven" from their homes (Ex 12.15). Paul warns that as "just a small amount of leaven ferments the entire lump of dough," so the influence of the incestuous man in their midst will inevitably pervade the church.[15] Others may imitate his boldness, and even those who do not will be negatively affected by having this kind of uncleanness in their midst. So just as Israel put away the old leaven, the Corinthians must remove this man from their midst. They are already late with this, Paul says: "For our Passover Lamb, Christ, has been sacrificed." The old leaven was to be removed before the slaying of the Passover lambs. Christ has already died for our sins, yet the Corinthian church has not purged out the old leaven. The time is long past for them to be tolerating such "leaven" in their midst.[16]

---

[13] Neither "shunning" nor "excommunication" is an inaccurate way to describe what Paul is talking about, but because of their common association with particular denominational contexts and the specific procedures that accompany them, they are avoided in this study. Note, however, that "disfellowship" is no more biblical a term than are the other two.

[14] Paul's use of "among you" in verses 1 and 2 shows that the entire church is implicated in the man's sin, since it is known "among them." Therefore it cannot be treated as a private matter (Garland, 159).

[15] Garland describes such sin as "a pestilent moral virus" that is likely to infect the entire church community (159).

[16] For further discussion of the imagery of leaven in Paul's letters, see C.L. Mitton,

(3) Verses 9–13 speak clearly of not associating with immoral people. Paul had addressed this problem in an earlier letter which we do not have and now clarifies that he was speaking specifically of not associating with those who call themselves our "brothers" yet live like pagans. They are "not even to eat with such a one" (v 12, ESV), which probably refers both to the Lord's Supper and to ordinary meals. In other words, such people should no longer enjoy the church's fellowship at any level.

(4) Verse 13 contains a commandment frequently found in Deuteronomy: "Drive out the wicked person from among you."[17] Through Moses, God emphatically instructed Israel to remove evil from their midst. In the same way, Paul uses these words to encourage the Corinthians to do likewise.

This is apparently a more complete and more severe action than what Paul had commanded the Thessalonians ("hold yourselves aloof from every brother who conducts himself in a disorderly manner" and "take notice of that person and do not associate with him"). In the situation at Corinth there is no warning him as a brother or any continual admonitions to do better. Nor do we find Paul recommending a three-step process of going to the sinner with a progressively wider circle of witnesses as in Matthew 18. This isn't to say that Paul is not concerned for the spiritual welfare of the incestuous man, since the ultimate goal is "so that the spirit may be saved in the day of the Lord." But the situation is a dangerous one for the entire church and requires them to take serious measures at once. When someone's house is on fire, we don't politely knock at the door. There is imminent danger, not only to the man himself but to the church, and his example has already im-

"New Wine in Old Wineskins: IV. Leaven," *Expository Times* 84 (1972/73), 339–43, and J.K. Howard, "Christ Our Passover: A Study of the Passover-Exodus Theme in I Corinthians," *Evangelical Quarterly* 41 (1969), 97–108.

[17] See Deuteronomy 13.6; 17.12; 19.13; 21.21; 22.21–22, 24; 24.7.

pacted them negatively. There are times when a church must act—and act quickly—in order to minimize the damage inflicted by a flagrantly sinning member. Our usual tendency is to act slowly, even in such drastic cases as Paul outlines in 1 Corinthians 5, for fear that we will act too hastily. Even when the circumstances are obvious and discipline is clearly required, we sometimes drag out the whole process to such lengths that irreparable and unnecessary damage is done while we try to decide what to do. However, it's difficult to imagine Paul cautioning the Corinthians not to act too quickly in this case.

As stated at the beginning of this chapter, the action prescribed in 1 Corinthians 5 isn't for every situation where discipline is required. But it *is* for cases of blatant and dangerous disregard for Christian morality, and we shouldn't hesitate to employ it when warranted. Delivering someone to Satan is indeed the radical surgery of church discipline, but there are times when, in the spiritual realm as in the physical, such surgery is exactly what's needed. It is impossible to calculate the damage caused by our failures (or slowness) to act in such situations, not only within congregations themselves but also by the defaming of the gospel and of the church which so often accompanies our failures to discipline appropriately.

But How Do We Know When?

How do we determine when a situation calls for such drastic (and rapid) action? To some extent this must be left to the judgment of the church under the guidance of its leaders. Paul offers some specific help in verse 11 where he names some additional sins which might require severe corrective measures: sexual immorality, greed, idolatry, slander, drunkenness, and theft. This list is likely representative and not intended to be exhaustive of all sins which might demand delivering someone to Satan. Rather, it points to the *types* of sins which require it. Notice that some sins in this list, such as greed and slander, are not ones which usually show up on our lists of more serious sins. But they betray deep-seated spiritual problems and can cause serious destruction to the church. Often the greatest havoc is wreaked in churches not by people who are flagrantly immoral but by people who exhibit ungodly attitudes of bitterness, hostility, jealousy, and selfish ambition. Yet these are almost never disciplined. Jesus provides another guideline in Matthew 18.15–17. Any fellow-Christian who stubbornly persists in a sin after being admonished repeatedly must eventually be dealt with by complete avoidance. Paul apparently doesn't go through the steps outlined in Matthew 18, not because he didn't know them as some suggest, but because the Corinthian situation is already well known to all and is too dangerous not to deal with speedily.

Wait a Minute…

What Paul calls for in 1 Corinthians 5 sounds so extreme to modern ears that it isn't surprising that we frequently hear strong objections to doing what he says, even when we acknowledge what it is he's telling us to do. Here are two of the most common objections:

(1) *"Such an action as Paul describes can only be construed as unloving and hurtful. The only hope of reforming a sinner is continued patience and a non-judgmental attitude toward his/her behavior."*

We've already noted that such a response betrays a decidedly unbiblical understanding of what love means, along with a lack of appreciation of the seriousness of sin. Real love cannot sit by and watch a loved one commit sins which will inevitably result in eternal condemnation without doing everything possible to prevent it. In the very next chapter of 1 Corinthians after he gives these instructions, Paul warns, "Do not be deceived; neither the sexually immoral, nor idolaters, nor adulterers, nor men who practice homosexuality, nor thieves, nor the greedy, nor drunkards, nor revilers, nor swindlers will inherit the kingdom of God" (6.9–10). As in the physical realm, so in the spiritual: when death is imminent, severe and painful measures may be unpleasant but are in no way unloving. The real love question is, do we love one another enough to take whatever action is necessary to bring about repentance?[18]

(2) *"How will withdrawing our fellowship from someone who is flagrantly sinning help the situation? Won't this just make matters worse and insure they will never return?"*

In 1 Corinthians 5.1–8, although Paul doesn't state it, he seems to assume that delivering someone to Satan will hopefully induce repentance, which will in turn lead to the salvation of the person's spirit on the day of the Lord. As in Jesus' instructions in Matthew 18.15–17, the hope is that the shock of being ostracized by the entire body of believers will cause the sinner to realize what he or she has lost in the present and what will be lost in eternity. Although this is Paul's stated goal, there is no guarantee of its effectiveness, since sinning believers continue to have free will just as do sinning non-believers. The sinning Christian may, in fact, become hardened in sin. In that case the salvation of the individual becomes secondary to the preservation of the church as a whole. The "old leaven" must be removed before it spoils the whole lump of dough. There is an element of trust involved here. Since these are the instructions that we have in the Scriptures, we must trust that in God's wisdom such measures will be effective

---

[18] It seems to me this is a question that we ought to ask ourselves in the selection of shepherds in our churches: "Does this man love me enough to do whatever it might take to save me from spiritual ruin should such a thing become necessary?" If the answer is "no," that man is not shepherd material. Shepherds don't let their sheep be slaughtered without doing everything they can to prevent it. But as we will see further, discipline isn't the responsibility only of shepherds.

when prayerfully and humbly employed. The refusal to engage in stringent disciplinary measures, even when Scripture clearly calls for them, is a sign of our mistrust of the word which God has given us, the only word we have for divine guidance. Perhaps we should speculate less about its wisdom and, as obedient children, find out what God can and will do when we conform to His word.

Discipline, Holiness, and Fellowship

By now the connections between the withdrawal of the church's fellowship and the larger concerns of holiness and congregational fellowship ought to be obvious. Without holiness no one will see the Lord (Heb 12.14), and discipline—even extreme discipline—is essential to the preservation of holiness. Paul's appeal to the leaven/Passover themes in 1 Corinthians 5 brings this out clearly. But such measures can only be effective where fellowship is vital and real, in churches where fellowship, once withdrawn, will be sorely missed and where brothers and sisters are genuinely pained to witness sin in each other's lives and are unwilling to ignore it. In such churches, where love prevails and holiness before God is of primary concern, even the most severe forms of godly discipline can and will be effective.

Additional Note:
A Critique of the Curse/Death View of Early
Christian Discipline

In the Additional Note attached to chapter 8, I explained that a significant number of New Testament scholars are convinced that early Christian discipline involved the use of curses which were expected to result in the death of the offender, as in many ancient Greek and Jewish curse formulas. According to this view, the primary goal of church discipline was simply to remove troublesome members who compromised the church's standards and identity. I've said enough already, I think, to demonstrate the inadequacy of this interpretation. Still, because 1 Corinthians 5.5 is so frequently interpreted in this way, it deserves further discussion. The curse/death interpretation of this verse maintains that "delivery to Satan" involved placing the offender under a curse and the "destruction of the flesh" signifies physical death, resulting in eventual salvation.[19]

This view must be rejected for the following reasons:[20]

(1) As noted earlier, the Greek and Jewish curse formulas which supposedly point to this interpretation are not genuine parallels to 1 Corinthians 5.5.

(2) Acts 5.1–11 and 1 Corinthians 11.30 are not parallel to 1 Corinthians 5.5, although they are frequently cited in support of the curse/death view. Both texts speak of people receiving "capital punishment" for spiritual offenses, but in both the deaths are punitive and not redemptive. Likewise neither of these texts says anything about the role of the assembled church which Paul requires in 1 Corinthians 5. The deaths which occurred in Acts 5 and 1 Corinthians 11 were the direct act of God and in no way the result of anyone being cursed by the church.

(3) The only New Testament verbal parallel to "deliver to Satan" excludes the idea of death. In 1 Timothy 1.20 Paul states that he had handed over Hymenaeus and Alexander to Satan "that they may learn not to blaspheme." They were not expected to die but to learn some-

---

[19] For examples of this point of view, see C.T. Craig, "The First Epistle to the Corinthians," *The Interpreter's Bible*, Vol. X (New York and Nashville: Abingdon, 1953), 62; Hans Conzelmann, *A Commentary on the First Epistle to the Corinthians* (Philadelphia: Fortress, 1975), 97; W.F. Orr and J.A. Walther, *The Anchor Bible: 1 Corinthians* (Garden City, New York: Doubleday, 1976), 186. Some believe the incestuous man was expected to die but do not connect this with a curse: C.K. Barrett, *The First Epistle to the Corinthians* (New York: Harper & Row, 1968), 126–27; F.F. Bruce, *1 and 2 Corinthians* (Grand Rapids: Eerdmans, 1971), 54–55.

[20] For a fuller discussion of the curse/death interpretation and its refutation, see South, *Disciplinary Practices in Pauline Texts*, 38–65; J.T. South, "A Critique of the Curse/Death Interpretation of 1 Corinthians 5.1–8," *New Testament Studies*, Vol. 39 No. 4, October, 1993, 539–61, and Anthony C. Thistleton, *The First Epistle to the Corinthians: A Commentary on the Greek Text* (Grand Rapids and Cambridge, U.K., 2000), 396–400.

thing from being disciplined. If the man in 1 Corinthians 5 was expected to die, what was he supposed to learn?[21]

(4) The curse/death view goes against Paul's usual use of the contrast between "the flesh" and "the spirit." The curse/death view requires that "destruction of the flesh" means physical death, leading to the salvation of the sinner. But when Paul contrasts "flesh" and "spirit" he is usually referring to different attitudes and orientations of life, not to a contrast between the soul and the body. (See Gal 3.3; 5.1, 16–26; 6.8; Rom 8.3–18.)

(5) As noted above, the context of 1 Corinthians 5.5 explains the meaning of "delivery to Satan": exclusion from fellowship (vv 2b, 9–13).

(6) The curse/death view cannot account for the fact that the offender is to be delivered to Satan "so that the spirit may be saved in the day of the Lord." It is entirely inconsistent with New Testament teaching to believe that one's own death could somehow atone for sins. Only the death of Christ has atoning power. If the works of the law could not bring justification and forgiveness (Gal 2.16; 3.10; Rom 3.20, etc.), how could one's own death, brought about by *sinful* behavior, possibly be expected to do so?

For Thought and Discussion

1. Why should we be cautious about using 1 Corinthians 5 as a normative text for all cases of church discipline?

2. What does Paul mean by "delivering someone to Satan"? Why do you think he uses such dramatic terminology? Why do you think we don't use this terminology today?

3. How does delivering someone to Satan differ from the kind of avoidance taught in 2 Thessalonians 3?

---

[21] As Richard E. Oster wryly observes, "How could Paul have hoped that this Christian might be saved at the time of Christ's return if he drops dead at the time the congregation hands him over to Satan?" (*The College Press NIV Commentary: 1 Corinthians* [Joplin, MO: College Press, 1995], 129).

4. Why doesn't Paul tell the Corinthians to "go through the steps" as outlined in Matthew 18.15–17? Are there times when this is not required or not advisable? Why or why not? If so, when might those times be?

5. Why does Paul include an attitudinal sin such as greed in his list of sins requiring discipline? Have you ever known of anyone being disciplined for this sin? If not, why do you think this is the case? How might it be effectively determined that someone is greedy?

ELEVEN

When a Brother Needs Forgiveness
2 Corinthians 2.5–11

Humanity is never so beautiful as when praying for forgiveness
or else forgiving another. (John Paul Richter)

It was a typical Sunday morning and the service had just gotten
under way when Bill walked in the back door and took a seat. We
were all caught off guard, and I remember my first thought as if
it were yesterday: "What does *he* want?" I later learned that most
of the small congregation felt much the same way. You see, only a
few months before Bill had boldly announced that he was leaving
his wife and two lovely children for another woman with whom
he'd been carrying on an illicit relationship for the past several
years. Despite the pleas of various members of the church and
the traumatic effect on his family, he moved in with the other
woman, right before the watching eyes of our small town. There
was only one course of action open to the church, and we took
it, not in a hostile way but with fear and trembling. In a meeting
of the entire church, after discussing the Bible's instructions on
discipline and our unsuccessful attempts to get Bill to change his
mind, we agreed that we must withdraw our fellowship from him
and formally did so the following Sunday.

Still, there was a great deal of anger in our hearts toward Bill. It was all so senseless and unnecessary and tragic. And he was so callous about it, even telling us defiantly that he would be disappointed if we did *not* disfellowship him. So when he walked in that Sunday morning just weeks later, he didn't find a group of people who were in a very forgiving mood.

At the close of the sermon, we found out what he wanted. He walked to the front of the auditorium during the invitation song, sat down on the front pew, and began to confess tearfully what a fool he had been. He had had everything any man could want but had thrown it all way. As he wept he acknowledged everything that we and his family had tried to tell him earlier. And he begged for God's forgiveness—and ours.

I'd like to report that we were overwhelmed with sympathy and compassion for our fallen brother, but it wasn't that easy. We accepted his statement of confession, but it took a while to even begin to really forgive him. We had become frozen in our anger toward Bill, so much so that, when he responded to God's discipline and to his own foolishness, we weren't ready to receive him back. After all, just look at the damage he had already done, we thought. Besides, none of us had really thought beyond the process of discipline. Once our fellowship had been withdrawn, that was the end of it. We had done all that God required. Or so we thought.

The Process Isn't Finished

Bill's story highlights an important truth about the church's fellowship, especially as it relates to the drastic breaches of fellowship that sometimes occur: *Disciplining an erring brother or sister is never an end in itself.* As we have seen in Matthew 18.15–17, the goal is restoration and forgiveness—not discipline. Discipline is merely the necessary means to a higher goal of restoring someone to fellowship with God and His people as well as of protecting the church from destructive influences. And whenever we enter into a process of disciplinary action, whether as individuals or as a congregation, we should already be thinking about the goal and looking forward to the healing of the broken relationship. Of course, we have no way of knowing in advance what the outcome of our efforts will be, but if we plan only for the worst scenario, it is unlikely that we will experience the best. Entering into a disciplinary process with the attitude that it "won't do any good"—at least as far as achieving restoration is concerned—is much like evangelizing with the same assumption. We severely lessen the chances that it *will* "do any good" if we proceed with a negative attitude. Even if it does prove effective, we will be ill-prepared to capitalize on the positive results, and disaster will likely result because disaster is what we were expecting. *It is imperative that churches learn to discipline lovingly and with the expectation of positive results.* Otherwise we will continue to experience the disastrous results that all too often accompany discipline in various churches. Jesus taught plainly in Matthew 18 that the goal of lovingly confronting a sinning Christian is to "gain your brother." If our goal is less than that, it isn't likely that our efforts will be tempered with the right spirit that will encourage others to return to the Lord and to His people.

A Penitent Sinner at Corinth

The church at Corinth was confronted with a similar situation to the one I described earlier in this chapter. After considerable conflict and confusion, the church had expelled from its fellowship a man who had been sexually involved with his father's wife (1 Cor 5.1–13; see Chapter 10). As a result the man repented, and Paul wrote to instruct the church what to do then. That he needed to do so indicates that they, too, were having difficulty responding to a penitent brother. Here are Paul's instructions:

But if anyone has caused grief, he has not caused it to me, but to some extent—though I don't wish to be harsh—to all of you. For such a person this punishment by the majority is sufficient. But now in place of that you must forgive and comfort him, lest he be overwhelmed by excessive grief. Therefore I urge you to confirm your love for him. This is why I wrote, that I might know your character—that is, whether you are obedient in all things. Anyone whom you forgive of something, I forgive also. For indeed what I have forgiven, if I have forgiven anything, has been on your behalf in the presence of Christ, so that we may not be defrauded by Satan. For we are not ignorant of his schemes. (2 Cor 2.5–11; my translation)

Paul begins the body of 2 Corinthians with a defense of his travel plans, specifically explaining why he hadn't visited Corinth as expected (1.12ff). Apparently some were pointing to this failure to follow through with his intentions as evidence of Paul's unreliability and lack of integrity (1.15–22). But Paul explains that his failure to come had another motive altogether: he had wished to spare the Corinthians further pain by avoiding what he anticipated would be an unpleasant and fruitless confrontation with them (1.23–2.4).

It's at this point that we learn that there had already been such a painful and unproductive confrontation between Paul and the Corinthians, an occasion which Paul had followed with a letter of stinging rebuke. This visit and subsequent letter have come to be known as the "painful visit" and the "sorrowful letter." A later reference to the letter comes in 2 Corinthians 7.8, which shows it was not only written out of anguish but it likewise had produced considerable grief among the Corinthians when they read it. It becomes evident in 2.5–11 that the chief source of this friction between Paul and the Corinthians was a certain individual who had in some way caused offense. It is obvious from Paul's comments that this particular issue played a crucial role in the defense of his ministry (chs 1–7) and therefore was a central concern of the entire letter of 2 Corinthians. Paul speaks of the incident as well known to his readers so that the man and his offense require no further identification.

Now What?

Interestingly, 2 Corinthians 2.5–11 is the only text which addresses discipline after the fact. The church had already carried out Paul's instructions toward the offender, and their efforts had produced the desired result. What now?

Apparently in the Corinthians' minds, the offense which precipitated the "painful visit" and the "sorrowful letter" was primarily against Paul himself. Paul, however, seeks to dispel this notion by pointing out that the "pain" (or "sadness") was actually experienced by the entire church and was not uniquely or even primarily his. He downplays the personal element in order to focus on the real problem: the injury done to the church as a whole. In highlighting the broader effect of the offense, Paul shows sensitivity in not making the offender's guilt weigh any more heavily than necessary. The term *epibarein* ("to weigh down," "to burden") is peculiar to Paul in the New Testament[1] and is always metaphorical for a burden placed upon another. Paul doesn't want to over-burden the guilty party (who remains unnamed), but he wants the church to see that there is more involved here than a mere personal affront. Perhaps Paul knows they have been reluctant, as churches sometimes are, to recognize the whole affair as a communal problem. This failure to acknowledge the damage suffered by the church is part of the broader concern.

---

[1] The only other occurrences are in 1 Thessalonians 2.9 and 2 Thessalonians 3.8.

In verse 6 Paul pronounces the disciplinary action by the community as *hikanos*, "sufficient." This could mean either that it had gone on long enough or that it had been severe enough. The former is more likely since Paul says to end it, not alter it. The action is described as "this punishment."[2] The use of this term, coupled with Paul's plea for its reversal, strongly implies a formal act on the part of the church. The expression "by the majority" raises the possibility that the action was not a unanimous decision of the church and that there may have been a dissident minority. Note that 6.1–13 indicates there was still a pocket of resistance against Paul and his authority in the church at Corinth.

Because the punishment is "sufficient," another course of action is now called for (v 7). The offender now needs both forgiveness and comfort in order to prevent his being "overwhelmed" (or, perhaps, "drowned"—*katapino*) in an excess of grief over his sin and its consequences. The imagery of someone drowning in grief is striking, and Paul is concerned that the discipline not be carried beyond effectiveness to the point of vindictiveness. Its purpose has been accomplished, and if continued it could become destructive both for the offender as well as for the rest of the church. It's likely that Paul is afraid the offender might become so overwhelmed by his grief and by continual rebuke from the church that he will abandon his faith altogether. Note Paul's obvious concern, not just for the church, but for the offender's welfare as well. Even though he has been guilty of a serious sin and has brought considerable trouble to the congregation, he is not to be pruned or cast off in order to purify the church. The goal, once again, is to regain him, not to be rid of him.

---

[2] C.K. Barrett, *A Commentary on the Second Epistle to the Corinthians* (New York: Harper & Row, 1973), 90, objects to the translation of *epitimia* as "punishment," but this still seems the most natural translation. However, it is certainly possible to over-emphasize this aspect of discipline, as does Collins, *First Corinthians*, 207.

So Paul encourages the Corinthians to extend to the penitent offender a formal expression of their love and forgiveness (vv 7, 10). The verb *kyrosai* ("to confirm," "to ratify") often denotes the confirmation of a sale or the ratification of an appointment to office. Paul uses it again in Galatians 3.15 of the ratification of someone's will. He is apparently calling for a specific *act* of reaffirmation of the community's love for the offender to communicate that he still has a place among them. There must be no doubt in the man's mind that he has regained his place among his fellow believers.

"This is why I wrote" undoubtedly refers to the "sorrowful letter" mentioned in verse 3 rather than to 1 Corinthians. As painful as the "sorrowful letter" had been to write, it evidently had accomplished the desired effect. Its purpose was to serve as a test of their character, particularly of their willingness to be obedient "in all things" to Paul's authority as an apostle.

In verse 10 Paul shows his willingness to concur in the church's judgment regarding the now-penitent man. If they forgive him, Paul forgives him also. Once again he downplays the personal aspect of the offense by inserting "if I have forgiven anything" and by insisting that his forgiveness is not to satisfy any personal requirement on his part, but is "on your behalf in the presence of Christ." The first clause of verse 11 continues the thought of verse 10: Paul is willing to forgive whomever they forgive in order to prevent Satan from "defrauding"[3] the church. If both the church and Paul do not forgive the offender, Satan might cheat them of the opportunity for restoration and wholeness within their ranks. It is serious business to refuse to forgive when the time comes.

---

[3] This translation is preferable to RSV's "gaining the advantage over us" and NIV's "outwit us," because it fits better with Paul's use of *pleonekteo* ("take advantage of," "outwit," "defraud," "cheat") in 2 Corinthians 7.2 and 12.17–18. If they aren't careful, Satan may succeed in doing the very thing which some had accused Paul of doing—defrauding the church.

Stages in the Restoration of Fellowship

So what can we learn from this episode at Corinth about what is involved in restoring someone to fellowship after he has been disciplined by the church? Paul's words suggest three distinct stages in such restoration.

1. Forgiveness. In the case of the discipline at Corinth, Paul says now that the discipline has had its desired effect, "in place of that you must forgive...him" (v 7). Paul has already forgiven him (v 10), and now the church must follow his lead. His tone of urgency and exhortation suggests that he expects forgiveness not to come easily, and frequently it doesn't. Often in cases which require congregational discipline, there is plenty of anger and hard feelings. The process itself may be long and involved and may even create some dissension within the congregation, as it evidently was at Corinth. In the course of all this, it's easy to lose sight of the goal: to restore, not to punish. It's true that Paul refers to the church's discipline as "punishment" in verse 6, but he describes the punishment as "sufficient." Once repentance has occurred, the time for punishment and alienation is over. The withholding of fellowship is only a step in the process, not the ultimate goal. Now it's time for forgiveness. If we find that difficult, we need only think of all the times God has graciously forgiven us, and we don't deserve it any more or less than does our erring brother or sister. Forgiveness is an obligation, not an option.

2. Comfort. Once an erring believer has repented, the process is far from over for him or for the church. Even though forgiven by God and accepted back into the church's fellowship, both parties must still cope with the shame and embarrassment involved. So part of the restoration process is extending comfort as well as forgiveness (v 7). This might be accomplished in several ways. One would be by reassuring the individual that sinning and being disciplined does not make him any different from other Christians.[4] After all, Hebrews 12 reminds us that "the Lord disciplines those whom He loves." We are all in the process of being disciplined by God in order "that we may share His holiness" (Heb 12.10). That's why Paul cautions those who attempt to restore others to do so in a spirit of gentleness, "looking to yourself, lest you, too, be tempted" (Gal 6.1). In no way is this intended to make light of the penitent person's offense; it simply recognizes that we all are equally in need of God's grace. And what greater comfort could there be than to be reminded that God, who calls for our discipline, does so because of His gracious love? Restored sinners need to be reassured that God isn't finished with them simply because they have "blown it." After all, the Bible is filled with stories of people such as Moses, David, and Peter who "blew it" and yet were still loved and valued by God.

3. Confirmation of Love. "Therefore I urge you to confirm your love for him," Paul writes in verse 8. It's often said that one's penitence should be as public as one's sin; that is, if a person sins publicly, a public confession is in order. Whether or not that should be regarded as a rule, Paul certainly suggests that the church's confirmation of love should be as public as its discipline. In 2 Corinthians 2 he apparently calls for a specific *act* of reaffirmation of the church's love, as suggested by the use of the aorist infinitive *kyrosai* ("to confirm," "to ratify"; New English Bible: "I urge you therefore to assure him of your love for him by a formal act"). Alfred Plummer paraphrases verse 1 this way: "I therefore

---

[4] A possible exception to this would be in cases where the sin is something the person might be tempted to repeat and which could be harmful to others in the church, as in cases of child molestation or embezzlement. It isn't a good idea to put such people in place as children's teachers or church treasurers, which would only enhance the likelihood of temptation to repeat the offence. Those who have offended in such trusted roles and insist that, if truly forgiven, they should be trusted again, may not have repented at all. Penitent people don't make demands.

implore you to leave him no longer in suspense, but at once, by some formal act, put into execution, not any sentence of further punishment, but the renewal of your love for him."[5] By whatever means necessary, both formally as a collective body and individually, we must make it clear that our love for the penitent offender is as strong as ever. If done in the right spirit, discipline in no way will have diminished our love, and we must be prepared to demonstrate it.

And If We Don't...

Paul's admonitions to the church at Corinth also give ample warning of the serious consequences that can result if a church aborts the disciplinary process by failing to forgive and fully restore the sinner to fellowship.

1. The penitent person may be lost due to an overwhelming sense of guilt and grief. Paul urges forgiveness and comfort for the person who has sinned and repented "lest he be overwhelmed by excessive grief" (v 7). If discipline is carried beyond the point necessary to induce repentance, it becomes destructive. Penitent sinners who return to the body of Christ seeking restoration and forgiveness generally bear an enormous weight of guilt and shame. If they are not quickly confirmed by their brothers and sisters, they may abandon the faith entirely. Paul speaks of being overwhelmed by "excessive" grief, that is, more grief than necessary to bring about repentance. As noted above, the word translated "overwhelmed" (*katapino*) means to be swallowed up or drowned. The image of a penitent sinner drowning in excessive grief while the church stands by and refuses to offer its forgiveness and comfort is one which no congregation can bear to contemplate.

2. The church is guilty of disobedience. According to verse 9, Paul

[5] *A Critical and Exegetical Commentary on the Second Epistle of St. Paul to the Corinthians* (New York: Scribner's, 1915), 52.

had earlier written to the Corinthians regarding this matter, to see "whether you are obedient in all things." Initially his concern was their obedience in disciplining the immoral brother, something they were extremely reluctant to do (1 Cor 5.1–5). Now that they have complied, he wants them to be equally obedient in expressing their love and forgiveness. Extending forgiveness isn't an option, depending on how we happen to feel. In instructing the Corinthians to forgive, Paul reflects the teachings of Jesus, who taught His followers that forgiveness is required of all who wish to be His disciples. Just after Jesus taught His followers not to "write off" those who sin against them but to go to them personally and seek to regain them, Peter asked, "Lord, how often will my brother sin against me, and I forgive him? As many as seven times?" Jesus' reply must have shocked Peter: "I do not say to you seven times, but seventy times seven" (Matt 18.21–22). He followed this with the parable of the unmerciful servant and the declaration, "So also my heavenly Father will do to every one of you, if you do not forgive your brother from your heart" (18.35). The church is never at liberty to think we have "done our duty" by disciplining those who need it when we are unwilling to perform the corresponding duty of forgiveness.

3. Satan succeeds in defrauding the church. In verse 11 Paul explains that forgiveness and restoration are necessary "so that we may not be defrauded by Satan. For we are not ignorant of his schemes." Even in the act of disciplining those who sin, the church must never forget that Satan is always scheming against us, seeking ways to turn even holy actions to our destruction. If we discipline people and then refuse to reinstate them fully, we play right into his hands. Paul says we are "defrauded" by him. How? For one thing, whenever discipline occurs without forgiveness and reconciliation, Satan has an opportunity to promote tension and division within the church and to rob us of an opportunity for healing and growth. Even worse, however, he robs us of the soul of a brother or sister. What a tragedy for someone to be penitent and at the point of restoration, only to be rebuffed by a lack of loving forgiveness and be drowned in grief and give up the faith! We must remain painfully aware that the failure to act mercifully at this critical point in someone's life may result in Satan getting just what he wants.

At that critical moment in a Christian's life when sin gives way to godly sorrow, the church must respond with forgiveness, comfort, and confirmation of our love. Only then will we realize the benefits of godly discipline, both for our repenting brother or sister and for the body as a whole.

Additional Note:
Do 1 Corinthians 5 and 2 Corinthians 2 Describe the Same Instance of Discipline?

Until about the beginning of the 20th Century, scholars were virtually unanimous in identifying the incestuous man described in 1 Corinthians 5.1–8 with the man who needed forgiveness in 2 Corinthians 2.5–11. Since that time, however, the roster of those rejecting this view has become formidable, and their rejection is emphatic.[6] Those who follow the traditional view are few indeed.[7] Weighing the arguments

---

[6] These include, to name only a few, Paul Barnett, *The Second Epistle to the Corinthians* (Grand Rapids and Cambridge, U.K.: William B. Eerdmans Publishing Company, 1997); C.K. Barrett, *Essays on Paul* (Philadelphia: Westminster, 1982); Murray J. Harris, *The Second Epistle to the Corinthians: A Commentary on the Greek Text* (Grand Rapids: William B. Eerdmans Publishing Company, 2005); Rudolph Bultmann, *The Second Letter to the Corinthians* (Minneapolis: Augsburg, 1985; German edition, 1976); R. P. Martin, *Word Biblical Commentary: 2 Corinthians* (Waco, Texas: Word, 1986); R.V.G. Tasker, *The Second Epistle of Paul to the Corinthians* (Grand Rapids: William B. Eerdmans Publishing Company, 1958); F.F. Bruce, *1 and 2 Corinthians* (Grand Rapids: William B. Eerdmans Publishing Company, 1971); and James Thompson, *The Second Letter of Paul to the Corinthians* (Austin: Sweet Publishing, 1970).

[7] These include G.W.H. Lampe, "Church Discipline and the Interpretation of the Epistle to the Corinthians," in *Christian History and Interpretation* (Cambridge: University Press, 1967); P.E. Hughes, *Paul's Second Epistle to the Corinthians* (Grand Rapids:

on both sides, however, there still seem to be valid reasons for identifying the offender to be disciplined in 1 Corinthians 5 with the one to be forgiven in 2 Corinthians 2.

(1) Because of what Paul says in verses 5 and 10, most commentators conclude that the situation in 2 Corinthians 2 involves a personal insult to Paul concerning his authority as an apostle,[8] rather than the situation of sexual immorality discussed in 1 Corinthians 5. However, we should note that in these same verses Paul actually seeks to correct the Corinthians' assumption that he is the one who has been wronged. At the risk of further burdening the now-penitent offender, he emphasizes the corporate nature of the injury and denies that he is the injured party (v 5). Although he offers his personal forgiveness in verse 10, he also downplays its significance and focuses instead on the forgiveness which the church needs to express collectively. This corresponds well with the idea that the incestuous man in 1 Corinthians 5 was "leavening the whole lump" by his behavior. The case of incest was a test case of Paul's authority, and it may have been that the incestuous man took the lead in rejecting Paul on the occasion of his "painful visit" to Corinth (2 Cor 2.1), but the real damage was to the church itself. The incestuous man would have had ample reason to oppose Paul, simply because Paul was demanding that he be disciplined, and there may have been other factors at work as well, such as that the immoral man may also have been the leader of the "super spiritual" faction at Corinth.

(2) Beginning with Tertullian[9] in the early Third Century, scholars have raised the argument that Paul could not have so roundly condemned the man in 1 Corinthians 5 and then counseled his forgive-

---

William B. Eerdmans Publishing Company, 1962); and A.M.G. Stephenson, "A Defense of the Integrity of 2 Corinthians," in *The Authorship and Integrity of the New Testament* (London: S.P.C.K., 1965). Ernest Best, *Second Corinthians* (Atlanta: John Knox Press, 1987) is among the few who remain neutral on this question.

[8] Various theories are offered as to who the offender, if not the incestuous man of 1 Corinthians 5, might have been and why he opposed Paul. None are conclusive, however, since Paul simply doesn't say.

[9] *On Modesty*, 13.

ness in 2 Corinthians 2. The two requirements of discipline and for-giveness seem, from this perspective, to be mutually exclusive. But this exposes a fundamental misunderstanding of the purpose of the discipline commanded in 1 Corinthians 5. It wasn't merely for the of-fender's punishment—certainly not for his death, as many maintain—but "that his spirit may be saved in the day of the Lord Jesus," and 2 Corinthians 2.5–11 indicates the effectiveness of that action. Paul's fear in 2 Corinthians 2 that Satan might gain an advantage over or defraud the community is easily understood as taking the disciplinary action too far. The offender was delivered to Satan in order to motivate him to repentance and restoration, not to destroy or get rid of him. There is no conflict between the two actions of discipline and restoration; in fact, the one requires the other, according to Paul.

(3) Another frequent argument against the identification of the two offenders is that Paul mentions no sexual offense in 2 Corinthians 2. This is obviously true, but it is also true that he mentions no specific offense of *any* kind, not even one which constitutes a personal affront to himself. So this argument has little, if any force.

(4) There are certainly some differences between the two texts, such as the involvement of Satan in the discipline in 1 Corinthians 5 and the fear of his activity in 2 Corinthians 2. Still, we should not over-look the striking similarities. Both refer to Satan's activity in regard to discipline, both invoke the name of Jesus in solemn oaths, both dis-cuss communal discipline (yet to be accomplished in 1 Corinthians 5, almost completed in 2 Corinthians 2), and both require the church to act in obedience to apostolic authority. The differences do not by any means outweigh the similarities.

(5) In spite of the considerable arguments which are often made against the identification of the two offenders, there are two gener-ally overlooked questions which seem to support it. First, could Paul have written as he did in 2 Corinthians 2 unless the problem of the incestuous man had been satisfactorily resolved since his writing of 1 Corinthians 5? It is difficult to imagine him writing in such a concilia-tory tone as he does if that issue were still hanging in the air. There is

admittedly still tension between Paul and the Corinthians, but there is also a strong note of reconciliation (1.3–7; 3.3; 7.1–16). Could Paul have been proud, comforted, and joyful over a community that had failed to acknowledge his authority, was still puffed up with arrogance in spite of the outrageous sin in their midst, and had blatantly refused to obey his explicit commands? It hardly seems likely.

The second question is, if the problem outlined in 1 Corinthians 5 had been resolved successfully prior to the writing of 2 Corinthians, would Paul have written to them again without mentioning it? Would he have simply ignored the fact that so crucial an issue had been re-solved? Would he not rather have expressed his great relief and joy for the resolution of the problem in much the same terms that we find in 2 Corinthians? If 2 Corinthians 2 does not refer to the same incident as 1 Corinthians 5, it would seem necessary to postulate a resolution to the problem and an acknowledgement from Paul which took place in the interim between the writing of 1 and 2 Corinthians.[10]

Thoughtful consideration of these two questions, as well as of the other arguments presented above, would seem to tip the balance in favor of the identification of the two offenders. I conclude, therefore, that when Paul wrote concerning the man in need of forgiveness in 2 Corinthians 2, he was acknowledging the church's repentance of its first refusal (which is implied, if not stated, in v 9) to discipline the in-cestuous man and encouraging them to receive him back on the basis of his repentance.[11]

---

[10] Some writers reject the identification on the grounds that it requires 1 Corinthians to be regarded as the "sorrowful letter," which then led to the church's disciplining of the man and his subsequent repentance, whereas the identification of 1 Corinthians with the "sorrowful letter" seems highly unlikely. That 1 Corinthians was the "sorrowful letter" was the assumption of many writers from ancient times up until the beginning of the 20th Century, but it isn't necessary to the identification between the two incidents. There is no reason why the "sorrowful letter," following the writing of 1 Corinthians, could not have been the catalyst for the church's disciplinary action and the man's sub-sequent repentance, having been written precisely because the church had not obeyed Paul's earlier instructions in 1 Corinthians 5.

[11] Even if the two incidents are not the same, however, the points made above about the need to forgive and comfort those who repent still stand.

For Thought and Discussion

1. How does the expectation of either positive or negative results from our disciplinary efforts affect the outcome?

2. Comparing 2 Corinthians 2.5–11 to 1 Corinthians 5.1–8, do you agree or disagree that they discuss the same case of discipline? Why or why not? Does your conclusion affect your understanding of the need for forgiveness of those who repent after being disciplined?

3. What might a congregation do specifically to "make the restoration as public as the discipline" following someone's repentance?

4. Why are members of a church sometimes angry toward someone who has been disciplined? Is such anger justified? Why or why not?

5. Why is it important to remember Satan's schemes as we go about the practice of church discipline?

TWELVE

Disciplining the Domineering
3 John 9–10; Titus 3.10–11

Diotrephes is the father of a long line of sons who have not
learned to distinguish between love for Christ and His Church
and love for their own place in it. (Anonymous)

Frank was an intelligent man, a graduate of a Christian university,
well versed in the Bible, and a deacon in the church. These might
all sound like favorable qualities, but Frank used them in a very
manipulative fashion. Most of the members of the blue-collar
congregation, including the elders, were intimidated by his edu-
cation, knowledge, and intellect. So when he spoke, everyone felt
compelled to listen. And he spoke often. Every time someone did
something he didn't like, Frank would complain to the elders and
confront the perceived offender with an accusation of "liberalism"
(his one-size-fits-all charge), which basically meant any position
or action he didn't like. (This was in spite of the fact that he held
some very peculiar and biblically questionable beliefs himself.)

This went on for years, and the church settled into a pattern of
inactivity for fear of arousing Frank's ire. Any time he objected to
something, it was stopped, no matter how effective, productive, or
helpful it might have been. As a result the congregation was domi-

nated by one man's opinions on just about everything. The situation was deadening in its effect, but no one seemed to know what to do about it, and many didn't even realize what was taking place or the degree to which Frank's selfish outlook was hindering the church's life and service. So to keep the peace, no one said or did anything. After many years of this, a young minister came along who didn't know any better, and he openly challenged Frank on several occasions. This gave the elders courage, and they, too, began resisting Frank's domineering ways and refused to allow him to control the church any longer. Finding that he could no longer bluster his way over others, he shortly left for another congregation, only to begin the same destructive pattern of behavior all over again.

So Many "Franks"!

In trying to think of an example of such domination, it was difficult to select just one, because unfortunately the church never seems to lack its "Franks"—people with controlling personalities who care more about getting their way than about the welfare of the church or even about the will of God. Such people bully, threaten, sow seeds of discord, spread rumors, make accusations, and complain, all with a single goal in mind: getting their way. Sadly, because we are not accustomed to the practice of church discipline in other matters, we seldom know how to deal with a "Frank." And so these cantankerous and destructive people go on year after year dominating the churches they attend, stifling good works, exhausting the leadership, intimidating good people into silence, and generally depressing the church and forming it into their own image.

But there's no reason for this to happen. In fact, it isn't right to sit idly by and watch any man or woman dominate the Lord's people in such a negative fashion, particularly since the Scriptures give ample guidance in how to deal with them. It's time we wake up and acknowledge that much of our efforts at "keeping the peace" in the face of someone like Frank is in reality *a direct disobedience to biblical teachings.*

In this chapter we will examine a text from John and one from Paul which speak directly to the problem I've been describing: dealing with the domineering in a disciplinary way. These people are highly dangerous, and it isn't surprising that both writers discuss them in a very straightforward manner and encourage their readers (us included) to deal with them likewise.

Third John 9–10: Dealing with Diotrephes

We can't be certain who "Gaius" was (3 John 1), to whom John addressed his third letter, or where the church of which he was a member was located. But we know they had someone very much like Frank to deal with. In his deeply personal note to Gaius, John said that he had written to the church but that a man named Diotrephes was opposing his teaching and creating considerable trouble in the congregation:

> I wrote something to the church, but the would-be leader Diotrephes refuses to acknowledge us. So if I come, I will bring up the things he is doing, bringing ridiculous charges against us with malicious words. And as if that were not enough, he refuses to welcome the brothers himself and forbids those who want to do so and casts them out of the church. (3 John 9–10, my translation)

The problem evidently centered around the need for early churches to show hospitality to traveling missionaries, a service which Gaius had performed in a commendable way (vv 5–8). John had written to the entire congregation about this, but Diotrephes refused such instruction and prevented others from fulfilling their duty, even to the point of "disfellowshipping" those who defied him. His reasons? First, John says, he "loves to put himself first,"[1] indicating that he had his own desires and not the best interests of the church or the gospel at heart.[2] In other words he wanted to have his own way, even if it meant putting an obstacle in the way of Christian charity and the spreading of the gospel. Second, he was not above soiling the reputation of John, perhaps by means of rumor and back-stabbing accusation, in order to maintain control.

John had no intention of letting this pass; he would deal with Diotrephes personally when (he says "if," as though he isn't certain he will have opportunity to do so) he came to visit the church (v 10). We might wish that John had been a bit more specific about what he intended to do, but the important point for our purposes is that he had no intention of letting Diotrephes get by with his words and actions—not because they were personally painful to John but because Diotrephes, like Frank, was standing in the way of the progress of the gospel, and that couldn't be tolerated. This is a profound lesson for churches and their leaders today: we have no biblical warrant for standing by and watching someone like Di-

---

[1] Robert W. Yarbrough appropriately translates John's description of Diotrephes as "that status-loving Diotrephes" (*1–3 John* [Grand Rapids, Michigan: Baker Academic, 2008], 377). B.F. Westcott labels this section of the letter "the temporary triumph of ambition" (*The Epistles of St. John* [Grand Rapids: William B. Eerdmans Publishing Company; third edition 1892; Eerdmans edition 1966], 239). He adds, "There is nothing to indicate that Diotrephes held false opinions: his ambition only is blamed" (240).

[2] "The language suggests a self-promoted demagogue rather than a constitutional *presbyteros* or *episkopos*" (F.F. Bruce, *The Epistles of John* [Grand Rapids: William B. Eerdmans Publishing Company, 1970], 152). However, it should be noted that Diotrephes' attitude and actions would have been wrong even if he *had* been a duly-appointed leader. John Painter suggests that Diotrephes may have been the householder in whose home the church met so that he was able to expel those who disagreed with him, even without being an appointed leader (*1, 2, and 3 John* [Collegeville, Minnesota: The Liturgical Press, 2002], 373–74). Peter Rhea Jones, on the other hand, thinks that, since Diotrephes could pressure the church to "excommunicate" those who disagreed with him, he likely wielded considerable authority and was perhaps "the head of the church" (*1, 2, & 3 John* [Macon, Georgia: Smyth & Helwys, 2009], 273).

otrephes keep the church from being and doing what God's word clearly indicates He wants us to be and do, and we have John's clear statement that ignoring the situation isn't the way to handle it.

Notice the characteristics and activities of Diotrephes, which are frequently true of domineering people in churches today:

1. He had his own agenda for the church, even though it meant hindering the spread of the gospel.

2. He refused to acknowledge any authority but his own.

3. He used malicious words as a weapon against those who stood up to him.

4. He put a stop to the good works of others because of his own rebellious and ambitious spirit.

5. He wanted to "de-church" everyone who refused to agree with him and yield to his threats.

Sounds a lot like Frank, doesn't he? Not only does John intend to deal with him, but he also encourages Gaius not to be swayed by him but rather to imitate the good works of people such as Demetrius (vv 11–12). The worst thing we can do with a Diotrephes (or a Frank) is to allow him to stop us from doing the good which we would otherwise do. Such people can be notoriously difficult to stand up to, but it can and must be done.

On a practical note, although John doesn't mention it, once someone like Diotrephes encounters serious opposition, especially from a church's leaders, he (or she) most often won't stay around long. Since having their way means everything to such people, when they can no longer have it, the thrill is gone, and they will seek another audience (i.e., another group to manipulate). *This makes the practice of disciplining domineering people all the more important.* It probably won't take much to send them on their way, but if nothing is done, the situation will likely never change until they die or decide to move on to spread their poison elsewhere.

Back to the question of how to deal with such people, our next text from Paul offers the specific guidelines that John omits.

Titus 3.10–11: De-Fusing the Divisive

Just as John writes to Gaius about Diotrephes, so Paul writes to Titus in the context of his work among the churches on the island of Crete (Tit 1.5). It was a difficult work, one made more difficult by the presence of false teaching (1.9-10ff), a local tendency toward laziness and lack of self-control (1.12–13), and a quarrelsome spirit (3.9). Concerning the latter, Paul urges Titus to "avoid foolish controversies, genealogies, dissensions, and quarrels about the law, for they are unprofitable and worthless." Scholars offer numerous suggestions concerning the exact nature of these controversial issues,[3] but regardless of their specific content Paul labels them as "foolish" (or "stupid," as in RSV) and counsels Titus to "avoid" them.[4] As for those who insist on promoting such controversies, he says,

> Reject a divisive person after a first and second warning, knowing that such a person is perverted and is sinning and stands self-condemned. (3.10–11; my translation)

A legitimate question at this point is whether the people Titus had to deal with were merely creating problems over their opinions on various matters or were false teachers who promoted doctrines contrary to the gospel and to apostolic teaching. Some would draw a distinction between someone like Diotrephes, who was "merely opinionated," and a false teacher, who clearly teaches something contrary to revealed truth. In many churches a "Frank" would be tolerated indefinitely, but someone who believes something con-

---

[3] See, for example, the suggestions in G.W. Knight III, *The Pastoral Epistles* (Grand Rapids: William B. Eerdmans Publishing Company, 1992) and Donald Guthrie, *The Pastoral Epistles* (Grand Rapids: William B. Eerdmans Publishing Company, 1957).

[4] Literally, "go around them" (*perihistemi*).

sidered to be false or unbiblical would be quickly labeled, if not ostracized altogether. But is such a distinction warranted? The problem in Titus 3.10–11 seems to be not with any specific doctrine being contradicted or a falsehood being promoted. Rather, it speaks of the general attitude and divisiveness of those who enjoy controversies and the quarrels which so often accompany them.

Paul labels this kind of person as a *hairetikos*, which I have translated "a divisive person." The King James Version uses the word "heretick," which makes us think of someone who promotes doctrinal deviation, since that's what the English word "heretic" has come to mean. The Greek word is actually an adjective used as a noun and denotes someone who is part of a sect or faction (such as the "sects" of the Pharisees and Sadducees—Acts 5.17; 15.5— or even of the Nazarenes—Acts 24.5). It's concerned not so much with the truth or falsehood of what is believed as with the reality of creating a division among bodies of people.[5] This could be the result of teaching something contrary to Scripture, or it could simply involve the opinionated views, persistently advocated, by someone like Diotrephes or Frank. Titus 3.9 says nothing specific about the content of these teachings as far as truth or falsehood, only about the stupidity and controversial nature of the quarrels themselves.[6] This by no means suggests that false teaching may not be involved in such quarrels. Given the overall context of the letter to Titus, it very likely was.[7] But Paul's concern seems to be

---

[5] Most of the more recent translations reflect this understanding of the term: "divisive" (NIV); "factious" (NASB, RSV); "contentious" (REB); "any one who causes divisions" (NRSV); "a person who stirs up division" (ESV).

[6] As one example among many, our church once had to deal with a man who insisted that it was erroneous to refer to the Lord's Supper as "communion." In spite of our telling him he was free not to call it that but had to leave others free to disagree, he persisted in teaching others that they were sinning by not doing as he did.

[7] This is assumed by most commentators. See, for example, Knight (353–54), Guthrie (208); William Hendriksen, *New Testament Commentary: Exposition of the Pastoral Epistles* (Grand Rapids: Baker, 1957), 395; and Philip H. Towner, *The Letters to Timo-*

not so much doctrinal as practical: the discussions themselves are "unprofitable and worthless." A person who would promote such quarrels must be dealt with decisively because he/she poses a serious threat to the unity and overall health of the church.

So what are we to do with someone who creates disunity through foolish controversies? Paul says to give him two warnings and then "reject" him. Since he is still a brother in Christ, we must try to turn him away from his sinful behavior; therefore he must be warned of the consequences of his actions and attitude.[8] But because of the extreme danger he poses to the well-being of the church, the warning process must not continue indefinitely. Two warnings are the maximum allowed, but the fact that there are two also indicates a minimum number of warnings.[9] If both warnings fail to bring about the desired result (silence, at least), then the person must be rejected. It may be that the words of Jesus in Matthew 18.15–18 require at least these two warnings, but it should be noted that Paul doesn't require exactly the same procedure as outlined by the Lord. Perhaps this is because of the imminent danger posed by one who would, for the sake of his/her own opinions, threaten the peace and unity of the church.[10]

---

thy and Titus (Grand Rapids: William B. Eerdmans Publishing Company, 2006), 796. Although Guthrie adds, "The Greek word *hairetikos* translated *heretick* does not mean what the word 'heretic' means today. It designates one whom Simpson describes as 'an opinionative propagandist who promotes dissension by his pertinacity.' In later times the word acquired a more technical meaning of 'one who holds false doctrine'" (208).

[8] Towner suggests that the protracted nature of the process has in mind the recovery of the offender and believes that Paul's instructions are modeled on Matthew 18.15–17 (797).

[9] RSV obscures this by translating as "once or twice," suggesting there is an option of giving only a single warning. However, Paul's words literally read "after a first and second warning." "The advice given in 3.10 shows in its own way the limits of the power of words. A teacher of sound doctrine should engage in dialogue with false teachers. But he should not continue disputes" (Risto Saarinen, *The Pastoral Epistles with Philemon & Jude* [Grand Rapids, Michigan: Brazos Press, 2008], 194).

[10] "From the standpoint of the community ... the danger lies ... in fragmentation

To press a bit further, what is involved in this "rejection" of the divisive person? The verb *paraiteomai* is somewhat vague and means generally "to decline," "reject," or "refuse." It suggests at the least staying away from and refusing to be influenced by someone creating division. At the most it might mean a formal withdrawal of the church's fellowship.[11] Drawing on the text from 3 John, we can well imagine John coming to the congregation where Diotrephes was asserting himself and warning the church to stay away from him. We can equally imagine him encouraging the church to withdraw fellowship from him entirely, depending on his further attitudes and actions after being warned of his sin. Once again we note that Paul does not feel compelled to spell out for the church how far its discipline should go. He is mostly concerned with damage control where such people are concerned, whether that requires individual avoidance or a more formal congregational action, but under no circumstances can such a person simply be ignored.

The reason for such decisive action lies not only in the nature of the divisive person's actions but in his very nature: "knowing that such a person is perverted and is sinning and stands self-condemned" (v 11). To take delight in creating dissension and to be so determined to have one's own way is not only sinful but also perverted. Unfortunately, there are people who take a perverse delight in controversy. Usually disguising their warped motives as a quest for doctrinal purity, they are quick to engage in a fight over almost anything, just as Paul suggests in verse 9. Even when warned by the church at large or by its leaders, they refuse to desist and frequently respond with slander and malicious words

and resultant instability, which becomes particularly acute if the faction actively proselytizes within the larger community" (Towner, 797). He adds that it also poses a danger to the public image of the church.

[11] Towner (797) is certain it means exclusion from the congregation.

rather than face up to their own sin. Paul's sad verdict applies to such people today as much as it did in his own time: they stand self-condemned by their actions. Their very refusal to consider the peace of the church or the feelings and opinions of others and their willingness to engage in unwarranted verbal assaults reveals their true character. Unfortunately, "Franks" seldom repent.[12]

The words of Paul and John are a warning to all of us. The disruptive and divisive among us must be recognized for what they are and dealt with accordingly. Otherwise, disaster is sure to result. If such people are allowed to have their way, the church will languish under their domination and fail to do the good works which God has laid before us. Or we may become so embroiled in silly arguments about phony "issues" that all of our energies are sapped and we have nothing of substance to say to the unbelievers around us. Such disunity may lead to division at great cost to all involved. But godly discipline, lovingly but boldly administered, can prevent all of this and enable the church to move ahead unhindered by the pettiness of a domineering brother or sister. Genuine fellowship demands that we not ignore the destructive potential of someone like Frank. And our quest for God's holiness requires us to press on in our service to Him without the unholy influence and paralyzing arrogance of misguided people.

---

[12] Acknowledging the difficulty that peace-loving believers have in entering into controversy with such divisive people, R. Kent Hughes and Bryan Chapell point out that "there is a difference between needing to divide and loving to divide ... A person who loves the peace and purity of the church may be forced into division, but it is not his character" (*1 & 2 Timothy and Titus: To Guard the Deposit* [Wheaton, Illinois: Crossway Books, 2000], 364.

For Thought and Discussion

1. Have you personally known someone like Frank? What was his (or her) impact on the congregation as a whole? Was anything ever done to control the negative influence of this person? Why or why not?

2. Why do you think churches are so often intimidated and reluctant to deal with someone like Diotrephes or the divisive people described in Titus 3.10–11?

3. In what ways can people sometimes be divisive without actually teaching false doctrine? What specific examples can you think of?

4. How are people such as those discussed in this chapter usually dealt with in your congregation? What, if anything, do you think needs to change in regard to the treatment of such people?

5. Why do people such as Diotrephes so seldom repent? How does this serve as a warning to the rest of us?

THIRTEEN

Watching out for False Teachers
Romans 16.17–18

> There is a kind of peace which can be had at the cost of evading
> all issues, refusing all decisions, shutting the eyes to things that
> are crying out to be dealt with, a peace which comes of a lethar-
> gic inactivity and an avoidance of all decisive action. The Chris-
> tian must ever remember that the peace of God is not the peace
> which has submitted to the world, but the peace which has over-
> come the world. (William Barclay, *The Letter to the Romans*)

Acts 20.17–38 describes a particularly poignant meeting between
Paul and his long-time friends, the elders of the church at Ephesus. Paul had lived and worked among them for three years and
had a profound affection for them, an affection which they ar-
dently returned. As Paul prepared to leave for Jerusalem, he was
certain he would never see them again (vv 37–38), and so he gave
this prophetic warning:

> Pay careful attention to yourselves and to all the flock, in which
> the Holy Spirit has made you overseers, to care for the church of
> God, which he obtained with his own blood. I know that after
> My departure fierce wolves will come in among you, not spar-
> ing the flock, and from among your own selves will arise men

speaking twisted things, to draw away the disciples after them. Therefore be alert.... (Acts 20.28–31, ESV)

The New Testament is replete with warnings against the presence of false teaching in the church. In the case of Paul's warnings to the Ephesian elders, false teaching could arise from either (or both) of two sources, those "who will come in among you" and/or "from among your own selves." Jesus Himself gave such warnings (Matt 24.4–8, etc.), and the threat of false teaching is never very far from the minds of the inspired writers of the various letters.[1] But in spite of these warnings churches are often caught off guard when false teaching arises and as a result are unprepared to deal with it in a constructive and helpful manner. And left unchecked, unhealthy (the opposite of the healthy or "sound" teaching enjoined by Paul in 1 and 2 Timothy) teaching leads to unhealthy living and unhealthy churches and possibly even to spiritual destruction.

The Christian faith survives and thrives on teaching, but that teaching must promote spiritual health and vigorous life within the body of Christ. Not just anything will do. Far too often churches and their leaders are more attuned to secondary issues among believers and fail to notice when genuine false teachings which have the potential of eroding faith are being circulated. When we compare the matters which are often the object of quarreling and division among and within churches today to the great themes of the gospel, it becomes evident that we are too often majoring in minors and ignoring genuine heresy right under our noses.[2]

---

[1] See Rom 3.8; 1 Cor 15.12–19; Gal 1.8–9, 3.1; Eph 5.6; Phil 3.2; Col 2.8; 2 Thess 2.1; 1 Tim 1.3, 4.1; 2 Tim 4.1; Tit 1.10; 2 Pet 2.1, 3.3; 1 John 2.18, 4.1; 2 John 9–11; Jude 8; etc.

[2] Church leaders in particular would do well to study such texts as Eph 4.1–16, Col 2.6–23, and 1 John 2.18–25 to see the kind of concerns for healthy teaching that are expressed in Scripture and compare them with the issues that divide believers today.

Because of the seriousness of this situation, the Scriptures give us not only warnings about false teachers but also instructions for dealing with them in order to prevent them from wreaking havoc on the body of Christ. We need to acquaint ourselves and our congregations with these instructions *before* the fact, so that when circumstances require it we are prepared to exercise the needed discipline in an effective manner.

Watch Out!

Near the close of his letter to the church at Rome, Paul offered this warning:

> But I encourage you, brothers, to watch out for those who cause dissensions and hindrances in opposition to the teaching which you learned; turn away from them. For such people do not serve our Lord Christ; they serve their own bellies. And by means of smooth talk and flattery they are deceiving the hearts of those who don't know any better. (Romans 16.17–18; my translation)

At the time he wrote this historic letter, Paul had never been to Rome (Rom 1.13–15). However, that didn't mean he didn't know anyone in the church there. To the contrary, the final chapter indicates that he knew a surprisingly large number of people. In fact, he spends the first sixteen verses of Romans 16 giving greetings and commendations to a large number of friends and acquaintances, something he normally didn't do in his letters. Several reasons have been proposed as to why he does so toward the end of Romans, but regardless of his motives the important fact is that all of those he greeted were people who had been faithful to the apostolic message that he preached.

Although most translations don't indicate it, verse 17 actually begins with the word "but," as in my translation above.[3] What

---

[3] ESV, RSV, and NIV leave the *de* ("but") untranslated. NASB has "Now I urge you,

Paul is doing is *deliberately excluding* false teachers from the greeting extended to the faithful in verses 1–16. Although he does not use the word *koinonia* in this context, fellowship is the general topic of verses 3–23. Those who are fellow-believers and fellow-workers are greeted in the Lord. But those who disrupt that unity by their self-focused teachings are to receive a different kind of treatment entirely.

Paul's description of those not to be greeted makes it clear that the offenders are false teachers of some sort and not merely opinionated or domineering people such as those discussed in Chapter 12, since he identifies them as "those who cause dissensions and hindrances *in opposition to the teaching which you learned*." While it's impossible to determine with any certainty who they were or the exact nature of their falsehood, it's obvious they were teaching things which were in conflict with the gospel message that the Romans had received. Verse 18 reveals their motive: rather than serving Christ, they serve "their own bellies"—that is, their own fleshly appetites and desires. Likewise Paul asserts that they are not above using flattery and deceit in order to gain an audience for their views. Here we have an important insight into the motive behind much false teaching: a perverse desire for attention or an effort to gain a personal following. The same tendency is reflected in Paul's warning to the Ephesian elders that the "wolves" would seek "to draw away the disciples *after them*" (Acts 20.30). As is evident from Paul's statement and from experience, not all "doctrinal" disputes are really about doctrine.

What To Do?

Rather than a church being helpless in the face of self-centered false teachers, Paul tells us exactly what to do. He uses two terms to designate the necessary actions. The first is *skopeo*, which

brethren...." None of these do justice to the adversative force of *de*.

158 | *Church Discipline*

I have translated "watch out for" and which signifies critical observation of someone or something. It isn't an inherently negative
term,[4] as Philippians 3.17 shows: "Brothers, join in imitating me,
and keep your eyes on those who walk according to the example
you have in us" (ESV). This verse is in a sense the positive coun-
terpart of Romans 16.17. Just as the Romans must "watch out for"
false teachers, so the Philippians are advised to "keep your eyes
on" positive examples of Christian living and service. The King
James translation of *skopeo* as "mark" has led to the unfortunate
practice of branding people with labels such as "false teacher,"
"liberal," etc. In reality sometimes the real point of dispute is simply that they disagree with the one affixing the label. The verb in
no way justifies slandering a brother or sister, regardless of what
they believe or teach.

But Paul doesn't merely counsel his readers to observe troublesome teachers; he also says to "turn away from them." I have
chosen "turn away from" rather than the usual "avoid" (ESV, RSV)
to translate the verb *ekklino* because the Greek term implies a
deliberate rejection of a person (Rom 16.17), of evil conduct (1
Pet 3.11), or of righteous conduct (3.12). What would such a
rejection involve? It could be nothing more than my personally
refusing to talk to someone about his pet views. Or it might go
further and take the form of a formal action by the church as
a whole, depending on the false teacher's persistence and the
pervasiveness of his or her influence. Turning away from such a
person could be either a warning to the whole church not to be
influenced by their views or even a complete withdrawal of the
church's fellowship. Again, by not specifying exactly the action

---

[4] *Skopeo* is used outside the New Testament to describe the critical observation of
the judge, the philosopher, and the historian. For the variety of uses of this word and its
compound forms see E. Fuchs, *"skopeo," Theological Dictionary of the New Testament, Vol
7*, ed. by G. Friedrich and G.W. Bromiley (Grand Rapids, Michigan: William B. Eerdmans Publishing Company, 1971), 414–15.

to be taken, Paul leaves the Romans (and, by extension, us) free to tailor the action to suit the need.

Notice that Paul says nothing about giving two warnings, as in Titus 3.10–11, or about going to the false teacher privately and then in the company of witnesses, as in Matthew 18.15–17. In fact he says nothing at all about seeking to restore the false teacher. This seems somewhat contradictory to his words in 2 Timothy 2.24–26:

> And a servant of the Lord is not required to fight but to be kind to all, to be capable of teaching, to be forbearing, to correct opponents with gentleness, since God may grant to them repentance leading to knowledge of the truth and that they may come to their senses and escape the devil's snare, having been captured by him to do his will. (my translation)

These softer words likewise stand in sharp contrast to Philippians 3.2, where Paul warns against the influence of "Judaizers," Jewish Christians who taught that Gentiles must be circumcised in order to be saved. "Look out for the dogs, look out for the evildoers, look out for the mutilators!" How do we reconcile these texts? The most likely explanation is that the false teachers Paul has in view in Romans 16.17 and Philippians 3.2 are not part of the church but trouble-makers who may be expected to come in (or have already come in) from outside the community.[5] On the other hand, the "opponents" of 2 Timothy 2 are most likely Christians who have strayed into error, "having been captured by him [Satan] to do his will." The one circumstance requires

---

[5] On the basis of verse 19 most commentators favor the view that such false teachers were not yet in Rome. See, for example, W. Sanday and A.C. Headlam, *A Critical and Exegetical Commentary on the Epistle to the Romans* (Edinburgh: T. & T. Clark, 5th Edition, 1977), 429; also Leon Morris, *The Epistle to the Romans* (Grand Rapids, Michigan: William B. Eerdmans Publishing Company, 1988), 539.

staunch defense against theological invasion from outside, while the other requires gentle teaching and correction. Comparing 2 Timothy 2.24–26 with Titus 3.10–11, there is no reason why the "first and second warnings," which Paul requires in the case of the divisive individual (apparently a fellow Christian) in Titus 3, cannot be done with the gentle and forbearing spirit required by 2 Timothy 2. The point of Titus 3 seems to be that we should not be *too* forbearing in the case of someone whose perversity of mind can be a serious danger to the peace of the church. Again, as we have seen previously, the controlling principle is to suit the action to the need.[6]

Our Common Responsibility

It's important to note to whom Paul is speaking when he gives these instructions in Romans 16.17–20. He speaks in the second person plural, indicating that it is *everyone's* responsibility to be discerning about the teachings we hear and to avoid those who would lead us astray. In the same way, John cautions all of his readers not to believe every spirit but to "test the spirits to see whether they are from God" (1 John 4.1). In the "Letters to the Seven Churches" (Rev 2–3), the risen Christ scolds two of the congregations—Pergamum (Rev 2.12–17) and Thyatira (2.18–29)— for tolerating people in their midst who promoted false teaching and false living. Only a minority of those in these churches were guilty of false teaching, but the entire membership of both are held responsible for their failure to act to correct the situation. By contrast, the church at Ephesus, in spite of its other problems, has "tested those who call themselves apostles but are not, and found

---

[6] 1 John 2.19 contains an important reminder that not everyone who appears to be part of the fellowship actually is. Our fellowship, as John makes clear in 1.1–4, is based on our common faith, and it is not impossible to have those in our midst who, while outwardly holding church membership, do not in reality share our faith.

them to be false" (Rev 2.2). To quote John, "He who has an ear, let him hear what the Spirit says to the churches" (Rev 3.22).

Sadly, the tendency prevalent at Pergamum and Thyatira is too often our tendency also. It's much easier simply to turn a blind eye and a deaf ear to doctrinal deviations than it is to confront them. It's often the case that Christians will be disturbed by false teachings in their midst but will sit idly by and wonder why "someone" doesn't do something. We do this, I think, because it's just easier not to rock the boat than to raise the alarm about something which may be dangerous and harmful. Also we often buy into the common cultural mentality that "doctrine" isn't all that important, and we certainly don't want anyone thinking we take such things too seriously. Some believers are so fearful of the label of "narrow-minded" that they will tolerate almost any teaching rather than risk appearing to be that way. Likewise, sometimes those teaching falsely are influential people in the church because of their leadership positions, wealth, or long-standing membership[7]. Sadly, one of the most common reasons we don't discipline false teachers is because so many Christians simply don't know Scripture well enough to recognize false teaching when they hear it.

"Between Two Fires"

A young Ukrainian friend who was trying to refine her English skills once asked me the meaning of the saying, "between a rock and a hard place." I explained to her that it describes a situation in which a person doesn't seem to have any options that aren't difficult or that don't lead to further difficulties. Once she grasped the concept, she replied that Ukrainians have a similar descriptive phrase for such situations: "between two fires."

---

[7] Some suggest that this was the reason the Corinthians had failed to do anything about the incestuous man in their midst (1 Cor 5.1–8). It's possible that he was the leader of the faction that opposed Paul in the church.

When it comes to dealing with doctrinal deviations, we are often caught between two fires. On the one hand there is the fire of ignoring false teaching and allowing it to corrupt the faith of believers and weaken the health of the church. On the other there is the danger of developing a search-and-destroy mentality by which we're always on the lookout for falsehood in the beliefs of others so that we can sound the alarm to those around us. After all, Scripture teaches us to be alert and vigilant against that which is not true to the gospel, but at the same time we are to maintain the unity of the Spirit in the bond of peace and be kind and encouraging to all. How do we do both? Allow me to make a few suggestions:

1. *Recognize that not all beliefs are of equal importance.* When Paul wrote to the Corinthians about the resurrection of the dead, he identified as of "first importance" such things as the death, burial, and resurrection of Jesus (1 Cor 15.3ff). Obviously this suggests that there is a difference between these faith convictions and beliefs that are of "second importance," that is, not central to the gospel message. Likewise the "seven ones" of Ephesians 4.4–6 are truths which all believers presumably must hold in common: one body, one Spirit, one hope, one Lord, one faith, one baptism, and one God. But there are other matters which don't fall under any of these headings, and on these there will always be disagreements among believers. Paul discusses some of these in Romans 14.1–15.7 and in 1 Corinthians 8–10. They include such issues as dietary scruples and the observance of certain special days. Read closely and you'll see that Paul doesn't attempt to determine who is right and who is wrong in these matters; what he is most concerned about is *how they treat each other* as they attempt to resolve their disputes or as they simply learn to live with the fact that they don't agree. He nowhere indicates that they must decide right and wrong on every question about which they disagree, and if

someone holds a view which is potentially divisive or harmful if expressed, he is instructed to keep it between himself and God (Rom 14.22). But above all, believers must not pass judgment on one another about such secondary concerns. As long as someone isn't creating a problem over some personal point of view, there is no need for discipline. On the other hand, even a matter of secondary (or less) importance can become divisive and dangerous if it is pressed unnecessarily and may then call for the discipline of the church, as explained in Chapter 12.

The mere fact that Paul devotes so much space to these matters of opinion in Romans and 1 Corinthians shows that, while not things of first importance, they were nevertheless deeply important to his readers. What this tells us is that not everything about which we feel strongly is a matter of first importance, and we must beware of the tendency to flatten Scripture so that every matter discussed in it becomes of equal significance to the point that we are ready to go to war over any and every disagreement. There is a legitimate sphere of disagreement among Christians about many things, and we need to respect this biblical principle even as we watch out for false teachers.

When the New Testament speaks about false teaching, the context usually makes clear that the concern is with the central truths of the gospel, not with more peripheral matters. This provides us with a strong clue about which matters should concern us in a disciplinary way and which should not. Unfortunately, we sometimes lose perspective on such matters and are more ready to discipline (or label) someone with whom we disagree over a concern that is purely secondary to the gospel than we are to confront a genuinely false teacher. We've all seen situations in which more heat was generated over the appropriate use of church funds, for instance, than over the nature of Christ or the contents of the gospel. Recognizing that not all beliefs are equally significant should help us avoid such tragedies.

2. *Observe the congregational context of all church discipline.* In the era during which the New Testament was written, the church existed as independent local bodies of believers with no organizational ties among churches and no hierarchical structure governing all of them. That being the case, Scripture always speaks of discipline as needing to be carried out on the congregational level. In our study of discipline we have not uncovered a single instance in which someone is instructed to exercise discipline on a multi-congregational level and certainly not by spreading accusations against someone among multiple churches. In some instances the churches are told to practice individual avoidance, and in others congregation-wide action is necessary. We might even find it necessary on occasion to warn a church which is being invaded by someone who has a track record of creating "dissensions and hindrances" in other places (as Paul may have been doing with the Romans). But this must always be done discreetly, and no one is authorized by any of these texts to become doctrine police for the church at large. Such efforts are not uncommon, and while they may be well-intentioned, they are also seriously misguided. Keeping discipline within the family (the local church), will go a long way toward keeping us from becoming busy-bodies and gossips who do more harm than good. Besides, if we're paying attention to the needs of our own congregation, we won't have either the time for or the interest in policing the beliefs and activities of others. Having an inordinate interest in what's being done and said in other places may be a signal that we aren't paying sufficient attention to what's going on at home.

3. *Remember that, whenever possible, discipline should begin with personal confrontation.* As we've seen in the case of 1 Corinthi-

ans 5.1–8, there are times when starting discipline with a personal confrontation is neither desirable nor necessary. If everyone already knows the problem and the threat level is high for the church, it's best to act on a congregational level right away. On the other hand, Jesus said, "When you brother sins, go and tell him his fault between you and him alone." But for some reason, when the sin (or perceived sin) is of a doctrinal nature, some believe they are free (perhaps even obligated) to broadcast word of it to anyone they choose, even if their information is second- or third-hand. Such a practice shows no regard at all for the brother we are supposed to be trying to regain. Also it disregards the fact that we may not know the actual facts about what someone has said or what he believes and may therefore be guilty of spreading a false report. And even though what our brother believes may be very different from what we have always heard and believed, if we were to sit down with him and discuss it, we might find that his point of view is as biblical as our own, if not more so. On the other hand our personal attention and concern may help our brother see that he is, in fact, in error and respond accordingly. Again, keeping discipline within the context of the local church makes this both workable and effective and also makes us less likely to criticize the beliefs of others without knowing them—or without knowing what we're talking about.

Somewhere between the two fires of tolerating every destructive teaching which comes along and making an issue of every disagreement lies a narrow ground of responsible spiritual discernment. It is that ground that Scripture calls us to occupy. The concerns of our faith are simply too great for us to fail to "test the spirits," but the consequences of being over-zealous about doctrinal purity are equally drastic for the peace and unity of the church.

The faith we hold in common is the basis for our fellowship, and we must guard that foundation at all costs while at the same time remembering that those with whom we disagree are our brothers and sisters. Likewise our identity as God's holy people requires us to be true to His word but also not to unnecessarily injure the body or any member of it in the process. It may be difficult to walk between two fires, but it's worth it in order to remain true to our faith and to one another.

For Thought and Discussion

1. Explain in your own words why the discipline of false teachers should be on a congregational level rather than a multi-congregational level. Are there any exceptions to this principle? If so, what are they, and how might this be done in a way consistent with what Scripture teaches?

2. Provide some possible scenarios of rejecting a false teacher on both a personal and a congregational level. Be as specific as possible in describing what might be done.

3. Why does Paul not discuss warning false teachers before rejecting them in Romans 16.17? Is this inconsistent with his teachings elsewhere?

4. What suggestions can you add to the list of ways to reject false teaching without developing a search-and-destroy mentality?

5. Do you think churches generally are more likely to discipline people for moral failure or for doctrinal error? Explain why you think so.

FOURTEEN

"Re-Branding" the Role of Elders

First, then, in order to be a good shepherd, the Elder must exercise the utmost care to prevent individual sheep from straying away from the flock; and when one, as it sometimes will, eludes all vigilance and strays away, he is to be prompt and energetic in going out to search for it and bring it back. (J.W. McGarvey, *The Eldership*)

During an interview with a group of elders and deacons from a church of almost two thousand members, I asked if they practiced corrective discipline. I was stunned by the reply of one of the elders: "We've never needed to." His comment told me a great deal, not only about the church he represented but also about his concept of what elders are and what they're supposed to do. I'd like to think that his point of view is a rare one, but the evidence proves otherwise: it's painfully obvious in most churches that elders don't always see themselves as *shepherds* charged with the responsibility for the spiritual welfare of those in their care. As a result they frequently ignore circumstances that are crying out for corrective discipline, simply because the very idea isn't on their radar.

Many Labels, Same Men

Although some would disagree, it seems to me that the New Testament is clear that the earliest Christian communities had (and, by extension, that churches today ought to have) groups of men[1] who were chosen to oversee them not just materially and physically but especially spiritually. It also seems evident that these men were called by a variety of descriptive terms rather than by one formal title. For example, Acts 20.17–38 records an emotional meeting between Paul and the elders of the church in Ephesus. Paul was on his way to Jerusalem, where he would be subsequently arrested and eventually sent off to Rome, and he was quite sure he would never see his friends in Ephesus again. So he met with them, not just to say good-bye, but also to give some warnings about dangers that lay ahead. In verse 27 he said, "Pay careful attention to yourselves and to all the flock, in which the Holy Spirit has made you overseers, to care for the church of God, which he obtained with his own blood." Notice that these elders are also described as "overseers." The Greek term for "overseers" is *episkopoi*, which means those who watch out for or look over someone or something.[2] So it seems that elders were also known as "overseers" rather than these being two separate functions or different groups of people. This is affirmed by Titus 1.5–7 where *presbyteroi* ("elders") and *episkopos* (the singular of *episkopoi*) are used interchangeably. The former term means, literally, "older men." Combined with *episkopoi* it indicates that

---

[1] That they were men and not women is made clear in 1 Timothy 3.1–7 and Titus 1.5–9.

[2] It is sometimes translated as "bishop," but this isn't really helpful, since that term has come to mean something quite different than what Paul apparently intended—an ecclesiastical office-holder who has charge over several churches in several towns or cities. In the New Testament *episkopoi* seem always to have overseen only one congregation or perhaps more than one in a given city where there might be several house-churches meeting in various locations. In either case, they were strictly local leaders.

elders were older men who were appointed to oversee the needs of God's people in a given locality.

There is another indication of fluid terminology where elders are concerned, likewise found in Acts 20. Not only were the elders also overseers, but Paul charged them to "care for the church of God." "Care for" expresses a single word in Greek, *poimainein*, a verb sometimes translated as "shepherd" or "tend a flock." The implication is that these elders/overseers were also the church's "shepherds."[3] First Peter 5.1–5 confirms this, as Peter speaks to the "elders" of the church and, as did Paul, tells them to "shepherd (*poimanate*) the flock of God that is among you, exercising oversight (*episkopountes*).[4] So this verse brings all three designations of "elders," "overseers," and "shepherds" together. That Peter sees these elders as "under-shepherds" is further confirmed by his references to Jesus as "the chief Shepherd" in verse 4.[5]

The Forgotten Role

Somehow in our own times we have largely abandoned the notion that elders in the church should be shepherds, with all that such a designation implies. Shepherds look after the sheep, go af-

---

[3] "Pastor" is a legitimate translation of this term, but, like "bishop," it isn't a helpful one since it has come to mean one person who has responsibility and/or authority over a church and has become synonymous with "preacher" or "minister." These functions could all have been found in one person, but overseeing/shepherding and preaching aren't exactly the same.

[4] Note that this word is absent from some manuscripts and so does not appear in all English translations but does in the ESV.

[5] The admonition to "Obey your leaders and submit to them, for they are keeping watch over your souls, as those who will have to give an account" (Heb 13.17) does not specifically mention elders/overseers/shepherds. Nevertheless, it seems clear that these are the "leaders" (or at least some of them) in the author's mind, further cementing together the roles of elders as shepherds who have responsibility for the souls in their care. See the helpful discussion of the three terms for the same role in Everett Ferguson, *The Church of Christ: A Biblical Ecclesiology for Today* (Grand Rapids, MI: William B. Eerdmans Publishing Company, 1996), 318–326.

ter those who stray (as in Jesus' beautiful parables), feed and guide and give counsel. In other words, they are the ones specifically charged with the responsibility to take care of spiritual needs, *not* to serve as a board of directors who make decisions for the church. Decision-making is by necessity part of the shepherding process, but it should never be the focal point of the elders' role. As shepherds focus their attention primarily on sheep, shepherds of God's church should focus on *people*.

I'm happy to observe a renewed emphasis on elders serving as shepherds in many churches today. But still there is often a general absence of seeing discipline as part of the shepherding process. Several excellent books and articles are now available that highlight the biblical necessity for elders to shepherd the church, but noticeably absent from almost all of them is any consideration at all of the need for elders to lead the church in corrective discipline, in spite of all the New Testament has to say about the need for it. Clearly there needs to be considerably more study and thought devoted to the connection between shepherding the church and the practice of discipline. How likely is it that churches will ever return to the practice of corrective discipline if they are not *led* to do so by those who have the responsibility for the spiritual welfare of the people in them?[6] And why would Jesus and inspired writers such as Paul teach church discipline if people could be adequately shepherded without it?

Perhaps a re-examination of Jesus' teachings about shepherds might help move us in the right direction.[7]

---

[6] This is especially evident in the fact that before discipline can become part of the life of the church, people need to be taught its necessity and importance.

[7] While, as we have seen, there is no single biblical designation for elders, it might be helpful to use the term "shepherds" more frequently as a reminder both to the elders and the church as a whole of their true function.

The Good Shepherd and the Church's Shepherds

Oddly enough, when we study and teach on the subject of elders, we tend to focus mostly on the New Testament letters and very little, if at all, on the teachings of Jesus and the Old Testament background underlying them. But since Jesus identifies Himself in John 10.11 as "the good Shepherd," it seems that shepherds today should look to Him as their prime example (as implied in 1 Pet 5.1–5).

In John 10 Jesus identifies Himself as not only "the good shepherd" but also as "the door" of the sheepfold. Shepherds in ancient Israel frequently herded their sheep into either natural or man-made enclosures of stones or brush, then lay across the entrance to prevent any sheep from leaving or any predator from entering. So the shepherd was also the gate-keeper of the sheep and their safety. Here's a powerful metaphor for modern-day shepherds in the church: those who lay down their own lives to protect the people who look to them for leadership and guidance.

Notice that Jesus didn't say simply, "I am *a* good shepherd," but "I am *the* good shepherd." He seemed to have a particular "good shepherd" in mind when He said this. The background for the good shepherd concept lies in Ezekiel 34.1–24, an unforgettably powerful text in which God chastises the shepherds (i.e., princes and kings) of Israel for not taking care of the sheep (the people placed in their care). According to Ezekiel 34.2–4 they had fed themselves, not the sheep, and they had failed to strengthen the weak, heal the sick, bind up the wounded, and seek those who were lost. In other words, they had failed in just about every responsibility placed upon a shepherd. The result was that the sheep were scattered and exposed as food for the wild beasts (vv 5–6).

Beginning in verse 11 God says He will Himself shepherd the flock of Israel and, in verses 23–24, predicts the coming of "one shepherd, my servant David," who will feed the sheep and be the shepherd for them that Israel's leaders had failed to be. In John 10, then, Jesus claims to be *that shepherd*.[8] To demonstrate this (in the spirit of Ezek 34.1–24) He contrasts Himself with the "thieves and robbers" who falsely claim leadership and the "hirelings" who care nothing for the sheep and so neglect them when they're needed most. The goal of the Good Shepherd is "abundant life" for the sheep, and His method of attaining that goal is to lay down His own life for them.

Now a question: Who are the "thieves and robbers" and the "hirelings" Jesus speaks against in John 10? Contextually, the answer lies in John 9, where a man blind from birth had been seriously mistreated by the Pharisees because he refused to denounce Jesus. Jesus gave the man sight for the first time in his life. The Pharisees, rather than rejoicing over this, interrogated him and, when he didn't give the answers about Jesus that they wanted, threatened him and "cast him out" (i.e., expelled him from the synagogue; vv 22, 34). In no way had these supposed spiritual shepherds of the people helped this man, and they refused to acknowledge the identity and power of the One who did. They were the direct descendants of the worthless shepherds condemned in Ezekiel 34. So Jesus deliberately contrasted Himself with these Pharisees, people who enjoyed the prestige, titles, and places of honor reserved for spiritual leaders of the people, yet who failed to feed even one desperately needy sheep.

In doing so Jesus said the true shepherd knows his sheep and they know him and follow him wherever he leads them because they know he has their best interests at heart. At any time

---

[8] Note that His claim combines the concepts of the good shepherd foretold in Ezekiel with that of the Davidic Messiah to come (see 2 Sam 7.11–14). In the latter sense Jesus is "my servant David" who would be the good shepherd that Israel's shepherds had failed to be.

he is ready to put himself between them and danger, to ward off predators, to stand and fight for their survival rather than running to preserve his own. I cannot imagine a higher, nobler role model for those who would be shepherds of God's people today—or a more sober warning not to neglect the welfare of those placed in their care.

At times this will undoubtedly call for congregational discipline. Nothing could be more destructive to the sheep than for sin to be ignored and its leavening influence spread throughout the church, as Paul warned in 1 Corinthians 5.6–8. Likewise there will sometimes arise "wolves," either false teachers or simply destructive people whose unrestrained activities can leave a church lifeless and floundering unless they are identified and their influence removed or countered, as in Titus 3.10–11 and Romans 16.17–20. *There is simply no way that spiritual shepherds can effectively guard the church of God without occasionally taking disciplinary action.*

A Communal Responsibility

So does this mean that corrective discipline is primarily or exclusively the responsibility of elders in the church? Not at all. By now I hope you've noticed that the texts which speak of discipline *always address the church as a whole* and not just the elders or any other specific group within the congregation. No one is singled out in these texts as having the sole responsibility for corrective church discipline.

Let's review a bit. When Jesus spoke of discipline in Matthew 18.15–17, He instructed His disciples generally, "If your brother sins, go and tell him his fault. . . ." Every disciple of Jesus bears the responsibility to care enough for a sinning brother or sister to confront them lovingly when sin is apparent. And if the erring person cannot be regained by private effort, others are to be brought into the picture until finally the entire church is informed and enlisted in the effort to reclaim. And if the efforts of the entire group fail, it is everyone's responsibility to "let him be to you as a Gentile and a tax collector." It's essential that everyone, as far as possible, be involved in the attempt to restore and, if necessary, in the ostracism which both protects the church from further harm and hopefully will eventually turn the heart of the one disciplined.

In the same way Paul's consistent practice is to speak to the entire church about disciplinary needs, not just to the elders, ministers, or other leaders.[9] As we saw in our study of Galatians 6.1, "you who are spiritual" does not refer to a distinct group within the Galatian churches, but to the members of the churches themselves, all who are "walking by the Spirit" rather than yielding to the flesh. Likewise Paul holds the entire church at Corinth responsible for tolerating the incestuous man (1 Cor 5.1–8); in solemn assembly the church as a whole must "deliver him to Satan," and later, after he has repented, all must equally forgive him so that he doesn't come to worse spiritual harm (2 Cor 2.5–11). The entire church at Thessalonica also are called upon to keep away from the disorderly and to warn them of the consequences of their misconduct (1 Thess 5.14; 2 Thess 3.6–15). And the Roman church as a body is exhorted to watch out for and turn away from those whose teachings are in opposition to what they had already received (Rom 16.17–18).

The only exceptions to speaking to the church as a whole are those letters in which Paul addresses his associates Timothy and Titus. Here Paul naturally speaks to his apostolic delegates in the singular, but we should not conclude that there are people in the church today with the same authority to act unilaterally in regard to discipline or other matters. Timothy and Titus were

---

[9] Remember that it was the common practice for churches to read apostolic letters in worship assemblies, so that what was written was brought to the attention of the entire faith community.

Paul's personal representatives, sent by him to accomplish specific tasks (which in both cases probably necessitated discipline). Also the fact that these letters were preserved by the churches with which Titus and Timothy worked, and that the church today still regards them as normative for the church as a whole, suggests that discipline is, even in these letters, the concern of the entire body and not just its leaders. The same principle holds true in 1 John 4.1–6, in which John makes "testing the spirits" the obligation of the entire church. And when Jesus scolds the churches of Pergamum and Thyatira for their tolerance of false teachers and compromisers (Rev 2.12–29), He confronts the congregations as units (represented by their "angels")[10] and adds the solemn warning: "He who has an ear, let him hear what the Spirit says *to the churches*" (Rev 2.29; 3.6, 13, 22).

Leading in Discipline

So does this mean the elders have no special role in the exercise of corrective discipline? Obviously, that would be an erroneous and unrealistic conclusion. Common sense requires that someone must take the lead in corrective discipline, especially when it leads to actions on a congregational level (telling it to the church, warning against false teachers, etc.). Some very delicate decisions must be made in such cases, and who would be better suited to make them than the church's shepherds who are charged with

---

[10] A common interpretation of the "angels" of the seven churches is that they are the "pastors" (in the modern sense, not the biblical one noted above) of the individual churches (see, for example, Ray Summers, *Worthy Is the Lamb* [Nashville: Broadman, 1951], 105, 109). But it seems more likely that the "angels" in some sense represent the churches themselves, since it is clear in each letter that Christ is addressing the church as a whole, not just individual leaders. "The Jews had long since become accustomed to the idea that each nation had its angelic representative in heaven, who presided over its fortunes and was held accountable for its misdeeds, and John is simply adapting this familiar notion to a new situation" (G. B .Caird, *A Commentary on the Revelation of St. John the Divine* [London: Adam & Charles Black, 1966], 24).

the responsibility to look after the spiritual welfare of the entire congregation? It isn't wrong to look to the elders to provide such leadership; it *is* wrong to conclude that no action can be taken until it is taken by one or more of the elders. The texts discussed in previous chapters, especially Matthew 18.15–17 and Galatians 6.1, indicate that any of us can and should begin the effort to restore whenever we become aware of the need for intervention. But once the process has begun and a wider circle of intervention is called for, we would hope that the elders would take the lead in trying to reclaim a lost sheep.

Although no Scriptures make the elders *exclusively* responsible for discipline, there are biblical indications that they have a special responsibility in this regard. Remember that Paul told the elders at Ephesus to "Pay careful attention to yourselves and to all the flock, in which the Holy Spirit has made you overseers…" (Acts 20.28). It's the elders who are warned that fierce wolves will come in and that the church will require their protection as they "care for" ("shepherd") the church of God. Likewise Paul reminds Titus that he had left him in Crete to "appoint elders in every town" (Tit 1.5), and a few verses later states one of the primary reasons for doing so: "He must hold firm to the trustworthy word as taught, so that he may be able to give instruction in sound doctrine and also to rebuke those who contradict it" (v 9). The Cretan elders weren't appointed to act as the board of directors for the church, but to teach the faith and protect the church from troublesome false teachers. Although Paul doesn't specifically mention elders in giving Titus instructions about divisive people (Tit 3.10–11), it follows logically from the context of the letter (especially 1.5–11) that the elders should take the lead in this. Otherwise, who would decide that someone had become so opinionated as to pose a danger to the entire church?

And remember that Hebrews 13.17 teaches us to submit to our leaders "for they are keeping watch over your souls, as those who will have to give an account." Anyone who has the primary responsibility for the care of souls must of necessity have primary responsibility for discipline.

In our pluralistic age with so many strange teachings coming at us from all directions, churches can ill afford elders who are not also true shepherds. How tragic that so many churches appoint men as elders—and that so many men accept the role—with virtually no thought given to their suitability or willingness to lead the church in corrective discipline when necessary. It's little wonder that so many churches are slowly dying from within because of sinful circumstances unresolved and not dealt with over many years, while others are torn by division created by people who could and should have been silenced, if only there had been adequate, godly leadership to confront them. Elders today must stop the obsession with budgets and buildings and turn those matters over to other capable people, while they devote themselves to praying for, tending to, and when necessary correcting those in danger of wandering from Christ, and they should be influencing others to attend to these brothers and sisters as well. This isn't intended as a blanket indictment of elders, many of whom are doing their best to lead God's people as His word directs, but as a fervent plea for more elders to recognize their God-given role as shepherds, including the mandate for discipline. Churches are suffering from a serious neglect of discipline, and this is unlikely to change until elders begin to lead us in the right direction.

What If There Are No Elders?

All over the world there are churches which function with very little formal leadership structure. Some of these are small, declining congregations which may no longer be able to find men adequately qualified to fill the roles described in 1 Timothy 3.1–7 and Titus 1.5–9. Others are mission churches which simply haven't yet reached the level of maturity where such leaders have been able to emerge and be recognized by their brothers and sisters. In some cases older churches have gone so long without elders that appointing them is no longer a matter of priority, so they have none. So a question that frequently arises in connection with discipline is, "Can a church practice discipline if it has no elders?" Because many assume that the answer is no, many of these churches languish in troubled circumstances that could be resolved through corrective discipline.

As we have noted, corrective discipline is first of all an *individual* function and secondarily a *leadership* function. That being the case, a church or an individual Christian can practice discipline in the absence of elders. Actions such as going privately to speak to someone about his sin don't require anyone else's participation or input. And if it becomes necessary to take one or two others with us, that, too, can be accomplished without elder involvement. It may be more difficult to "tell it to the church" and withdraw fellowship from someone without the leadership of elders, but even this can be done effectively. Some of the most effective cases of corrective discipline that I have ever witnessed were carried out by churches, both here and abroad, that had no elders yet effectively managed to confront, discipline, and even restore sinning members. Naturally this requires that the church take their collective responsibility seriously and act in unison (not necessarily unanimously), but doing so certainly is possible. So we should never allow the absence of elders to deter us from practicing discipline whenever necessary.

An even more difficult question is what to do when there are elders but they refuse to act when circumstances clearly call for congregational discipline. What can individual Christians do if they are aware of sin and have done all they can to correct it, even to the point of bringing it to the attention of the elders, only to be ignored?

Remember from what we have seen that the collective responsibility of the congregation begins with the actions of concerned individuals. Such active expressions of concern about the spiritual welfare of our brothers and sisters ought to be taking place all the time, with no thought about what others will or won't do. And even if our elders refuse to act in a given situation, that doesn't prevent the individual from personally withholding fellowship from a sinning member or false teacher.[11] Again, it is vitally important that, except in the extreme kinds of cases noted in the preceding chapters, we not short-circuit the process described in Matthew 18. We should go personally and privately to the sinning brother or sister and then take others with us. By observing Jesus' guidelines, we will hopefully be prevented from acting hastily or unfairly. It will also help us know what we should do personally regardless of whether the process goes any further.[12]

A simple comparison might help us understand our personal responsibility where discipline is concerned. Suppose you are in a church that isn't very evangelistic, where the leaders place no premium on nor provide leadership for leading others to Christ. Would this excuse you from doing what you could to bring others to the Lord? Or suppose the church collectively fails to see

[11] Note that in Matthew 18.17 the phrase "to you" is singular. Some conclude that this requires *only* an individual action of "letting him be to you as a Gentile and tax collector." But this does not logically follow, since in the scenario envisioned by Jesus the entire congregation has already become involved in the problem. The singular "to you" merely emphasizes the responsibility of the individual believer—of *all* individual believers.

[12] It should be observed that Paul's instructions to Timothy and Titus concerning discipline do not presume the participation of others. Hopefully the whole church would follow their lead, but they can and must act regardless of what others do or do not do.

its obligation to help the poor? Does that mean you shouldn't do what you can to help them? To ask these questions is to answer them. In the same way, we must individually accept our responsibility for the spiritual welfare of our brothers or sisters regardless of what others do or don't do—even the elders. When this happens more in our churches, then perhaps more men will emerge as elders who are willing to lead in corrective discipline, because it's something in which they have been engaged already as part of the church's culture of concern and fellowship. Remember that where genuine fellowship exists discipline will follow naturally among all members. And such churches will produce godly leaders who know that one of their primary responsibilities is to enhance that fellowship and preserve the church's holiness through discipline.

Elders Are Not Exempt

Before leaving the subject of the role of elders/shepherds in discipline, we should give some attention to a text which is often overlooked both in discussions of discipline and of church leadership in general. In 1 Timothy 5.19–21 Paul instructs Timothy to

> Pay no attention to an accusation against an elder, except "on the evidence of two or three witnesses." Rebuke those who are sinning in the presence of all so that the rest will have fear. I charge you before God and Christ Jesus and the elect angels, to keep these (instructions) without bias, not playing any favorites. (my translation)

Here is a much-needed reminder that the elders themselves are subject to the discipline of the church. They are not part of a hierarchy who dispense discipline to the rest, but shepherds of the flock who are likewise accountable to the "Chief Shepherd"

(1 Pet 5.4) and to their brothers and sisters and who experience the same weaknesses and temptations as all other Christians. Therefore they, too, must be "shepherded," even to the point of discipline when necessary.

Paul's primary point in this context is that elders not be treated unfairly, since their role within the church places them in a vulnerable position as the objects of criticism and accusation. Following the Mosaic rule of "two or three witnesses" (Deut 19.15), random accusations of wrong-doing are to be ignored. Unfair criticisms are, unfortunately, inevitable, and if all of them were to be taken seriously, no one could possibly function as a shepherd. But it is a different matter when two or three confirm an accusation of wrong-doing. When an elder is sinning,[13] his behavior ought not to be ignored in deference to his position. No role of leadership in the church should be construed as a license for sinful behavior.[14]

Persistently sinning elders, Paul says, are to be rebuked "in the presence of all." The question is, "all of whom?" There are two possibilities: "in the presence of the whole church,"[15] or "in

---

[13] "Sinning" expresses a present active participle, denoting an on-going situation for which there has been no repentance, not something of which an elder was once guilty. This explains the ESV and RSV rendering, "As for those who persist in sin..." G. W. Knight III, however, thinks the participle signifies not persistent sin but present guilt, a distinction which in my opinion is difficult to sustain (*The Pastoral Epistles: A Commentary on the Greek Text* [Grand Rapids, MI: William B. Eerdmans Publishing Company, 1992], 236).

[14] Although Paul doesn't specify it, the same could certainly be said of ministers, deacons, teachers, missionaries, and everyone else within the body.

[15] Some translations bias our understanding of Paul's words by translating *enopion panton* ("in the presence of all") as "in public" (Revised English Bible) or "publicly" (Jerusalem Bible, NIV). Knight (236–37) and Donald Guthrie, *The Pastoral Epistles* (Grand Rapids, MI: William B. Eerdmans Publishing Company, 1957), 106, agree with this interpretation. Likewise, Philip H. Towner, *The Letters to Timothy & Titus* (Grand Rapids, MI: William B. Eerdmans Publishing Company, 2006) translates *enopion panton* as "publicly, that is, in the presence of the whole congregation" (371) and adds that public rebuke probably indicates that private intervention has not been successful. Far off the

the presence of all of the elders."[16] Likewise, does "the rest" who are to stand in fear as a result of this action mean "the rest of the church" or "the rest of the elders"? This isn't an easy question, nor is it an unimportant one. On the basis of context, since Paul's immediate topic of discussion is elders, I prefer the latter interpretation, although the language itself could go either way. But remember that the main point is that there is to be no partiality; elders' sins are to be taken no more lightly nor more seriously than those of other Christians. Assuming that the principles of Matthew 18.15–17 are to be followed in the case of elders just as of anyone else, then rebuking them in the presence of the whole church or in the presence of all the other elders should surely be preceded by attempts to restore them privately.[17] If "in the presence of all" means before the entire congregation, then we should conclude that the principles of Matthew 18 are being assumed by Paul, even though they are not stated. In the case of elders, as of every other Christian, the goal is restoration and healing. Their special role as shepherds does not exempt them

---

mark is Raymond Collins' translation of "Cross examine sinners in the presence of all," and his claim that Paul envisions a judicial setting "before the entire assembly" (*1 & 2 Timothy and Titus: A Commentary* [Louisvile/London: Westminster John Knox Press, 2002], 147).

[16] This is the translation favored by the majority of commentators including Walter Lock, *A Critical and Exegetical Commentary on the Pastoral Epistles* (Edinburgh: T. & T. Clark, 1924), 63; J. W. Roberts, *Letters to Timothy* (Austin, TX: Sweet, 1964), 60; A. T. Hanson, *The Pastoral Epistles* (Grand Rapids, MI: William B. Eerdmans Publishing Company, 1982), 102–03; and William Hendriksen, *New Testament Commentary: Exposition of the Pastoral Epistles* (Grand Rapids, MI: Baker, 1957), 183. Jerome Quinn and William C. Wacker, *The First and Second Letters to Timothy* (Grand Rapids, MI: William B. Eerdmans Publishing Company, 2000) translate "while all of the presbyters look on" (452–53). W. Hulitt Gloer, *Smyth & Helwys Bible Commentary: 1 & 2 Timothy and Titus* (Macon, GA: Smyth & Helwys, 2010) concludes, "Though 'all' may refer to all members of the church, the context seems to favor that both phrases refer to the elders" (188).

[17] I cannot agree with Hendriksen, who maintains that an elder's sin is to be "punished even more severely than that of others" (183). This seems to miss entirely Paul's point that there should be no partiality.

from such action, nor should the consideration due any brother or sister be withheld in their case.[18]

Shepherding the people of God in a local church can be an exhausting, time-consuming, frustrating, and often thankless task. Naturally it also has its share of rewards, but at best it's difficult business. What I have said in this chapter is in no way intended as a blanket indictment of these godly men who give of themselves to shepherd the Lord's people, but rather as an encouragement both to them and to the churches they serve to follow the example of the Good Shepherd—including the necessity of recovering those who wander away and of protecting the church from the impact of those who would otherwise wreak havoc in it. My prayer is that they will find in these pages the encouragement and instruction they so desperately need and seek.

For Thought and Discussion

1. Why do you think we so often overlook the importance of elders as shepherds, including their role in leading the church in discipline whenever necessary? What sorts of things do we usually think of elders doing other than shepherding?

2. When the church where you worship selects elders, is anything said about selecting men who can and will lead in discipline?

3. If elders are to lead the church in exercising congregational discipline, what is the responsibility of the rest of the church? How is this responsibility reflected in Paul's letters?

---

[18] J. Carl Laney, *A Guide to Church Discipline* (Minneapolis, Minnesota: Bethany House Publishers, 1985), 166–169 (including his "Church Discipline Flow Chart") draws a distinction between the appropriate discipline of a leader and that of a "layman," a distinction not observed in Scripture. While there may be some practical considerations to take into account in the case of leaders, the discipline they receive is basically the same as for any other member.

4. Imagine you are a member of a small church which has no elders, and a situation arises where someone needs to be disciplined publicly. How should the church go about doing so?

5. In what way does Paul show that elders are not exempt from being disciplined when necessary? Should their discipline be stricter than that of other members? Why or why not?

FIFTEEN

The Shepherd and the Wolf

I know that after my departure fierce wolves will come in among you, not sparing the sheep. … He who is a hired hand and not a shepherd, who does not own the sheep, sees the wolf coming and leaves the sheep and flees, and the wolf snatches them and scatters them. He flees because he is a hired hand and cares nothing for the sheep. (Acts 20.29; John 10.12–13)

"I guess I just don't know the difference between someone who needs discipline and someone who is just being disagreeable." This honest acknowledgement, coming from the heart of a shepherd who was completely stymied by a situation that was crying out for discipline, reflects one of the major causes of inaction by elders/shepherds when discipline is clearly required: uncertainty about who is really a "wolf," a special category of people who require discipline by the church. We are often so fearful of disciplining inappropriately that, regrettably, we do nothing at all, often with tragic consequences. When a literal, four-legged-and-fur wolf comes in among a flock of sheep, it isn't difficult to tell which one is the wolf. The sheep know immediately and instinctively flee from their natural predator. And even a blind shepherd can quickly differentiate between one of his own sheep and a wolf that is threatening them. It isn't that easy, however, when "wolves in sheep's clothing" come in among the church, and shepherds have to be especially discerning in order to tell the difference—but it *can* (and *must*) be done.

In the text from Acts 20 quoted above, Paul foresaw a time when "fierce wolves" would invade the church at Ephesus, and he wanted the elders to be prepared to deal with them. Likewise in John 10, Jesus drew a sharp contrast between a true shepherd, one who owns and cares for the sheep, and a hireling who cares nothing for them. The evidence of the difference is that the hireling runs when he sees the wolf approaching, while the shepherd does all he can to protect the sheep from harm. Notice that in both texts the shepherd's reaction—or lack of it—is a matter of life and death. The fierce wolves will "not spare the sheep," because that's the nature of a wolf—to destroy sheep. The hireling (non-)shepherd flees because he knows the wolf is dangerous and doesn't want to deal with it. The result is an unprotected flock subject to the ravages of whatever wolf happens to come along.

And make no mistake: wolves will inevitably come. What Paul said to the elders of Ephesus could be said to any group of shepherds today. The wolves *will come*, and if not confronted properly they *will* ravage the flock. They may appear in a variety of forms, which is what makes identifying them a challenge. But if we are not prepared to acknowledge that some Christians really turn out to be wolves and are therefore not ready to deal with them as Scripture teaches, the results will be disastrous. In our time, when churches often number in the hundreds (if not thousands) of members, the destructive influence of wolves may not be immediately evident; we just "lose some members" and move on until the next wolf comes along and takes some more. The burden of preventing such disasters from occurring rests today just where it rested when Paul spoke: with those appointed as the church's shepherds, those who, as Hebrews 13.17

describes them, "are keeping watch over your souls, as those who will have to give an account."

So shepherds today are confronted with only two choices, biblically speaking. They must either educate themselves to identify wolves and learn how to deal with them, or step aside and let others who care more for the sheep assume those roles. *Pretending to be a shepherd while refusing to confront the wolf is not an option.* One of the requirements for being appointed as a shepherd is the ability to identify a wolf and the willingness to confront one whenever necessary.

What a Wolf Is Not[1]

As stated by both Jesus and Paul, a wolf is one who "snatches and scatters" the sheep. In the context of John 9–10, as we saw in the previous chapter, the wolf represented the religious leaders in Jesus' day who failed to care for and protect a helpless soul under their care. In Acts 20 Paul's primary concern was the inroads of false teachings and the wolves who would introduce and disseminate them. In a church setting, a wolf is anyone who brings confusion and destruction to the church, rather than building it up.

So it's important to know what a wolf is not.

1. *A wolf isn't an immature Christian who needs to grow.* People who are new to the faith almost always have very limited understanding and may sometimes say and do things which create a degree of confusion within a congregation, or at least among a

---

[1] By now it should be obvious from the discussion of the various New Testament texts which discuss discipline that not everyone needing discipline can rightly be described as a wolf in the sense that both Jesus and Paul use this term. Many, perhaps most, are simply people who allow sin to dominate their lives and need to be brought back to Christ's way, not people whose actions create havoc in the church. However, we should remember that all sin—especially that which goes undisciplined—has a negative impact on the church (1 Cor 5.6). Also, those who may properly be designated as wolves seldom see themselves as setting out to "destroy the flock." On the contrary, they are usually confident that they are right and that the church would be better off if they got their way.

circle of their friends and acquaintances within it. However, once taught, such people will normally realize the inappropriateness of their words or actions and cease to create a problem. Even when people are entrenched in their opinions, we need not view them as problematic and certainly not as objects of discipline (see 1 Cor 8 and Paul's comments on the treatment of those whose consciences are "weak"). New Christians (and sometimes not so new ones) need to be allowed room to grow, even to make mistakes, and so are not subject to corrective congregational discipline, unless their conduct is actually sinful and they are unrepentant. Shepherds who know their sheep well will be able to tell the difference.

2. *A wolf isn't someone who happens to disagree with you.* All church leaders (not just elders) need to resist the temptation to become exasperated with people who simply don't see things the way they do. All of us should study and re-study Paul's words in Romans 14.1–15.7 to learn how to disagree in the Lord while continuing to love one another within the same body. There are a host of things about which we might disagree. None of them is unimportant, but not all are so important as to lead to division or require discipline. (See Eph 4.4–6 for examples of some things that *are* that important. Note how few of them there are.) Otherwise, discipline is not to be used to bludgeon someone into submission to our way of thinking or get rid of them if they won't submit.

3. *A wolf isn't a troublesome member who needs constant maintenance.* I'll never forget the words of a wise elder who once said concerning a particular member, "We all know he's a perpetual maintenance problem." While every Christian should make certain he doesn't fall into that category, every church has people who, due to their own lack of diligence, constantly need to be checked up on, encouraged to do better, and urged to become more involved in the ministries of the church that will help their

spiritual growth. Such people often require a great deal of patience, but they aren't wolves.

Someone has said that there are always three groups within any church: sheep, goats, and wolves. The sheep are willing to be led and usually create no difficulties for the leaders. The goats are difficult but not destructive people. *But wolves are those whose attitudes, actions, and/or teachings are genuinely destructive and who refuse correction.* It's important for shepherds of God's church to know the difference.

How to Spot a Wolf

Thankfully, the New Testament contains a number of texts that are helpful in the never-ending task of identifying a wolf and knowing to deal with one when we see it. What follows is a brief overview of these texts, some of which are discussed at greater length elsewhere in this book.[2]

Acts 20.28–30. When Paul warned the Ephesian elders about the coming of "fierce wolves," he further identified them as those who "speak twisted things." This may refer to false doctrinal teaching, or it could indicate any sort of divisive talk such as gossiping, lying, etc. One thing that is almost always characteristic of a wolf is the use of perverse speech to influence others negatively. James 3.1–4.12 contains a lengthy section discussing congregational strife, and it's not surprising that it opens with a stern warning about the destructive power of the tongue, since strife among believers almost always begins in the mouth. We should take seriously James' description of the tongue as "a fire, a world of unrighteousness. The tongue is set among our mem-

---

[2] There is by necessity some repetition here in the discussion of some of these texts, but it's important to read them in the context of identifying a wolf as well for what they teach about discipline generally.

bers, staining the whole body,[3] setting on fire the entire course of life, and set on fire by hell" (3.6).

Don't fail to notice the purpose of this twisted speech according to Acts 20.30: "to draw away the disciples after them." *Wolves are always looking for an audience and are seeking more affirmation than they are getting.* As a result they care more about themselves and their status and getting their own way than they do about the welfare of the church. It is the goal of gaining a following and of gaining status at the expense of the peace of the church that distinguishes a wolf from the categories of people mentioned above.

Notice that Paul says these wolves can come in from outside ("will come in among you") or arise from within ("from among your own selves"). Ironically, a shepherd can turn out to be a wolf, too.[4]

3 John 9–10. These two verses describe the most famous wolf in the Bible, or at least the most notable one whose name we know: Diotrephes. His very name has become synonymous with a strong-willed troublemaker.

Notice the characteristics of Diotrephes, because they describe almost all wolves:

1. *He had his own agenda for the church.* Note the contrast between verses 5–8 and verses 9–10. Gaius and others like him were attempting to encourage the spread of the gospel by offering support and encouragement to traveling missionaries. Diotrephes, on the other hand, "refuses to welcome the brothers." Why? John doesn't say, but most likely it was because their presence in the church took away some of Diotrephes' thunder as a would-be

---

[3] See James T. South, *Uncommon Sense: The Message of James for Dispossessed Believers* (DeWard, 2014), 97–98 for the idea that "members" and "body" in James 3.6 probably refer to the church rather than to our physical bodies.

[4] As a historical note, what Paul predicted concerning the church at Ephesus eventually came to pass, as attested in the letters of 1 and 2 Timothy, addressed to his apostolic delegate who was trying to correct the troublesome situation at Ephesus.

leader. Or it may simply have been that he wanted to be disagreeable, that he didn't like the way funds were being used for mission efforts, or any number of other causes. Regardless, he thought he knew what was best and was willing to wreck the peace of the church in order to get his way.

2. *He acknowledged no authority but his own.* John says he has written something for the whole church, but Diotrephes, "who likes to put himself first, does not acknowledge our authority." The arrogance and narcissistic ways of wolves convince them that even though everyone else disagrees with them, everyone else is simply wrong. They must have their way, or else the church will pay the price. Ironically, the reality is that if the wolves have their way, the church will pay a much *higher* price.

3. *He used slander to discredit those who disagreed with him.* Since he refused to acknowledge John's authority, Diotrephes "talked wicked nonsense" against him. In other words, he wanted to discredit John's message by discrediting the messenger. We can only imagine what sort of accusations Diotrephes may have made against John in an attempt to persuade others that he was the only one worth listening to.

4. *He stopped the good works of others because he couldn't control them.* According to verse 10, Diotrephes not only refused to welcome traveling missionaries himself but he "also stops those who want to." A sure sign of a wolf is the willingness to subvert (or at least try to) the ministries carried on by others. Why? Because they aren't his/her ideas and aren't something he/she can control. How did Diotrephes go about stopping what others were doing? John doesn't say, but most likely it was by using some sort of intimidation (see the next paragraph below), by turning others against these good works, or by labeling those carrying them out as defective in some way. Very likely he used a combination of

192 | *Church Discipline*

these tactics. Wolves usually do. The goal is to stop what one can't control; methods don't really matter.

5. *He "de-churched" anyone who disagreed with him.* In John's words, he "puts them out of the church." Since wolves have no qualms about the effects of their words and actions on other believers or on the church as a whole, they are more than ready simply to get rid of someone who stands up to them. That Diotrephes was able to do this suggests that he perhaps had some sort of formal leadership role in the congregation, but whether he did or not, he clearly was not above using intimidation to get his way.

Perhaps the most important thing to note here is that John had no intention of allowing Diotrephes to get away with his destructive activities. "If I come, I will bring up what he is doing." What wolves need most is someone who will stand up to them. Especially if the leaders of a church do so, and it becomes obvious that the wolf will not get his way, he will usually simply go elsewhere. More than anything else, wolves want an audience.

Titus 3.8–11. In writing to one of his associates who was dealing with a tough church situation on the island of Crete, Paul says that believers should "devote themselves to good works" rather than getting involved in foolish controversies. But what about those who refuse to major in good works and prefer instead to be controversial? According to Paul, these people (wolves) must be warned a maximum of two times, then rejected. Paul describes such a person as a *hairetikos* (literally, "divisive person," not necessarily a false teacher as suggested by the King James use of the word "heretick"). One doesn't have to teach falsehood in order to be divisive. It is equally possible to create division over personal opinions or pointless controversies. There never seems to be a shortage of people who have some pet issue they want to discuss *ad nauseum*. Why? Because it makes them seem especially knowledgeable or wise to know something that others don't know—even if it's wrong or pointless. That's why Paul instructs Titus to warn them one or two times, then "have nothing more to do with him."

Notice Paul's description of such people, given as an explanation of why it is fruitless to continue discussions with them: "such a person is warped and sinful; he is self-condemned." This is what sets a wolf apart from someone who simply has a difference of opinion: no amount of teaching, warning, or even pleading will cause them to see the destructiveness of their words and actions. In their twisted minds it is more important to win an argument or champion a distorted point of view than to preserve the peace of the church. That's why they must be dealt with decisively. It may be difficult for elders to acknowledge that someone is "warped and sinful," but some people are, and it's the elders' responsibility to face that reality and deal with it when required.

Matthew 7.13–20. Toward the end of the Sermon on the Mount, Jesus warned His followers of the coming of false prophets, described as "wolves in sheep's clothing." Linking this warning to what Jesus had just taught about the "narrow gate" and the "hard way" that leads to life (vv 13–14), it seems that these false prophets are those who want to widen the gate by teaching that salvation can come in some other way than faithfully submitting to the teachings of Christ.

How can such false prophets be recognized? How do we know when someone is presenting a truth we haven't heard before or a lie disguised as truth? Jesus said, "by their fruits." In other words, what is the outcome of their teaching? Does it make the church stronger or weaker? Does it clarify truth or does it create confusion? *Does it draw people closer to Christ or only closer to the teachers themselves?* Are these teachers zealous to protect the welfare of the

194 | *Church Discipline*

church, or are they willing to use the church as a means to their own ends? It isn't that hard to tell. Jesus said, "You *will* recognize them by their fruits." It may take a while, but careful observation will eventually reveal the truth about them.

Romans 16.17–18. Toward the close of his letter to the church at Rome, Paul gives a warning about "those who cause divisions and create difficulties contrary to the doctrine that you have been taught." These particular wolves, unlike those described in Titus 3.10–11, are without doubt false teachers, because what they teach is in opposition to apostolic teaching. Notice what else Paul says about them: they "do not serve our Lord Christ, but their own appetites." It's hard to miss the similarities between these people and Diotrephes, isn't it? Like him, they aren't interested in promoting the gospel; they're interested in promoting themselves. And they do so by use of smooth talk, flattery, and deception. In short, they are clearly wolves. The only thing Paul advises is to "watch out" for them. Be aware of them. Keep your eye on them. If they persist in their activities, "avoid them," which could mean simply personal avoidance and refusal to discuss their views or, more drastically, eviction from the church's fellowship entirely.

1 Timothy 1.3–7. At the outset of his first letter to Timothy, Paul identifies a serious problem that was actually two-pronged. There were people in the church at Ephesus (just as Paul had predicted in Acts 20) who promoted both false doctrines ("different" doctrines, i.e., not what Paul himself taught) and worthless discussions ("myths and endless genealogies"). Notice their motive: they want to be teachers, even though they are completely unqualified for the role. It is often the case that wolves become wolves because they desire leadership roles or positions of influence for which they are unsuited. Rather than abide by the church's judgment about their qualifications, they determine to promote themselves even at the expense of the church's welfare. This is the essence of a wolf: self-promotion regardless of the cost to the church. So Paul tells Timothy to confront them and warn them to stop. We can only assume that if they had failed to do so, further measures (such as withdrawal of fellowship) would have been necessary, but the wolves couldn't simply be ignored and allowed to create dissension in the church.

2 Timothy 2.14–19. It turns out that Diotrephes isn't the only New Testament wolf whose name we know. Paul mentions two more in this text: Hymenaeus and Philetus. These two, he says, had "swerved from the truth" by saying that the resurrection had already occurred.[5] While we don't know the exact nature of what these two were saying, we do know the effect: "They are upsetting the faith of some." Not only that, but their words and actions involved "irreverent babble" that actually produced *un*godliness, rather than leading people to be more like Christ. Any time someone's teachings lead people to be less Christ-like and they refuse to be corrected, that's a wolf.

Notice the consequences if people such as Hymenaeus and Philetus aren't rebuked: "their talk will spread like gangrene." The image of a gangrenous infection gradually eating away at the health of the church isn't a pretty one, but it's an accurate description of what happens when wolves are allowed to have their way. What shepherd could contemplate the reality of such a thing happening to the people under his care and do nothing about it?

Portrait of a Wolf

From these texts a consistent portrait of the wolf emerges. A wolf is someone who

---

[5] We can only assume that these two had some distorted view of the meaning of "the resurrection," perhaps that it was a "spiritual" event that could occur unseen in an individual's life, rather than an observable phenomenon.

1. Creates division and confusion, either by teaching error or by insisting on discussing some pointless issue.

2. Seeks to gain a following for him/herself, often by insisting on being recognized as a teacher or leader even though not qualified for such a role.

3. Exalts him/herself and is determined to have his/her own way, regardless of the cost to the church and even at the expense of truth itself.

4. Has no regard for the spiritual welfare of other believers, but only for personal aggrandizement.

5. Will disregard or seek to undermine the duly appointed leadership of the church in order to have his/her own way.

As all of the texts we have examined reveal, it's vitally important for someone to confront the wolf whenever it threatens the flock, and Jesus said that's the job of a shepherd. Those who find themselves in this role or who contemplate being in it need to accept confronting wolves as simply part of the job at hand. And they must educate those whose souls are in their care about the need for disciplining people who refuse to repent when confronted. Their concern isn't just budgets, buildings, and meetings. It's shepherding, and there will be times when every shepherd will have to confront the wolf. When this is done lovingly and consistently as required, the church will be spared a great deal of trauma and loss. In fact, many won't even know it has occurred, but they will be blessed by the peace and security that comes from having shepherds who truly watch over their souls and who know a wolf when they see one and refuse to run.

For Thought and Discussion

1. Have you ever personally encountered a wolf in the church? How did this person's activities compare with those described in the texts discussed in this chapter?

2. Describe in your own words the difference between a wolf and a sinner who needs to be brought to repentance. Would you approach one the same way as the other? Why or why not? If not, what would be the difference(s)?

3. With so many warnings given in the New Testament concerning the coming of wolves into the church, why do you think that confronting them isn't emphasized more in the selection of shepherds? How can this be corrected?

4. Based on what you read in the texts discussed above, is a shepherd the only one who can or should confront a wolf? Why or why not? What might be a circumstance when someone else might be called on to do this?

SIXTEEN

Some Q&A on Discipline

*To abandon discipline because it has sometimes been ill-adminis-
tered is as unwarranted as it would be to abandon worship on the
ground that it has sometimes been ill-conducted. The relaxation
of discipline has often more absurd results than ever attended its
excesses. (Geddes MacGregor, The Coming Reformation)*

Just so you'll know, I have no delusions that what I have said so
far will answer all the questions which anyone might ask about
the important subject of discipline. Circumstances requiring discipline can vary in many ways, and each situation must be dealt with
individually, sensitively, and with a great deal of prayer for God's
guidance. It's no wonder Jesus promised that whenever "two or
three" come together in order to restore fellowship with a fallen
brother or sister, He is there among us; we desperately *need* Him.
Even with the assurance of His presence in our hearts and ears, we
can be certain there will always be many variables in disciplinary
situations—and therefore there will likewise be many questions.

Two works with which I am familiar deal at length with a
variety of frequently-asked questions and generally do so quite
well, so I see need to repeat their efforts. I'm referring to J. Carl
Laney's *A Guide to Church Discipline*[1] and a booklet by Flavil R.

---

[1] Minneapolis: Bethany, 1985.

Yeakley, Jr., *Questions and Answers on Church Discipline*, whose cover describes it as "Biblical and practical answers to the 25 questions most frequently asked concerning church discipline in general and specifically concerning the case of Guinn vs. the Collinsville Church of Christ."[2] Both works address a variety of questions in a sensitive and thought-provoking way, and, although I don't always agree with their answers, I highly recommend them for your consideration.

Several of the questions posed by Laney and Yeakley have been covered already in previous chapters, so I won't go over that ground again here. In this chapter I want to discuss a select few questions which have not been previously addressed but which are of such practical importance that our study would be incomplete without dealing with them. Most of these require a considerable amount of thought, prayer, and study to answer adequately, and perhaps they demand above all an intimate knowledge of the particular situation under consideration and the people involved in it. What I offer here is by no means infallible or applicable to every similar situation but is rather a mixture of applied biblical principles, common sense (to me, anyway), and opinion. I hope you find them useful in stimulating your own thinking and practices where discipline is concerned.

1. "Does discipline really have a place in today's pluralistic society?"

If you've read the chapters which precede this one (and I certainly hope you have; this topic is too serious to get the cart before the horse), I think you can anticipate my response to this one. First, a word of explanation. Pluralism is the world view that says there is no such thing as absolute or universal truth; that is, nothing is true or right for everyone all of the time, but truth is what

---

[2] Broken Arrow, Oklahoma: Christian Communications, 1984.

the individual perceives it to be, and what is "right" can change depending on one's circumstances and changing point of view. So there can be many conflicting "truths" without any of them being absolutely "wrong." I think you can see what this does to the whole concept of sin: it no longer exists. Just as nothing is absolutely, universally true and/or right, so nothing (according to pluralism) is absolutely wrong—therefore nothing can be labeled as "sinful." In fact, some pluralists claim that the only sin is to say that someone else is wrong in what they say or do, a point of view entirely inconsistent with their own philosophy.

It doesn't take a lot of thinking or reading of Scripture to see that pluralism isn't Christian. In fact, it's decidedly *anti*-Christian, because it denies one of the foundational tenets of our faith: that we're all sinners in need of a Savior. So while pluralistic thinking would undoubtedly rule out church discipline, it would also rule out Christian faith in general.

Sadly, a great many churches have succumbed to the pluralistic way of thinking, mostly as a way of accommodating the tastes of the people they're trying to reach. So they no longer speak much (if at all) of sin and salvation, much less of discipline. As a result, they have blended into the pluralistic landscape to an alarming degree and have become part of the problem rather than the solution. While pluralism would definitely rule against discipline, biblical faith rules against pluralism. So we must decide which world view to follow: that of Jesus and all of the biblical writers, or that of our present age which is sinking into decay and confusion at an alarming rate.

Ironically, what we often fear most—that church discipline will alienate people outside of Christ whom we are trying to reach with the gospel—is often the reverse of the truth. People (many, not all) are looking for standards, something on which to build their lives. If all they see in churches is the same pluralistic mind-set to which they're accustomed in daily life, why should they give these churches any consideration at all? On the other hand, if they see that we stand for truth and morality and a higher quality of life than pluralism can provide, they may just be attracted to the message we should so desperately want them to hear. Discipline is perhaps the ultimate indication that we take seriously what we claim to believe.

So, yes, there is most certainly a place for discipline in a pluralistic world. In fact, by refusing to engage in it, we are at least tacitly giving approval to the pluralistic view that anything goes and nothing is "wrong enough" to cause any consternation among Christians. As stated earlier, the church that stands for anything stands for nothing.

2. "Doesn't Matthew 7.1 prohibit church discipline, since we are not to judge others?"

I addressed this question briefly in an earlier chapter, but it's so commonplace that it probably needs more attention. Jesus' command, "Judge not, that you be not judged," is one of the most misunderstood sayings in the Bible. Verses 2–5 show the concern is that we not be harsh or unloving in our judgments; in other words, "judge not" means "condemn not." You don't have to read very far in the Gospels to know Jesus never taught that we shouldn't be discerning about the rightness or wrongness of another person's behavior. In fact, in verse 6 Jesus admonishes us not to give dogs what is holy or cast our pearls before swine. This certainly implies the need for moral and spiritual discernment regarding those who might fall into these categories. In addition, other texts clearly teach that we are not only allowed, but obligated, to make such judgments. After admonishing the Corinthians not to associate with sinning fellow Christians, Paul writes, "For what have I to do with judging outsiders? *Is it not those inside the church whom you are to judge?*" (1 Cor 5.12; emphasis mine). Likewise 1 John 4.1–6 instructs believers not to believe every spirit (teaching) but to "test the spirits, to see if they are of God."

So not only are we *permitted* to judge the behavior and teachings of others, we are *required* to do so, but always in a spirit of mercy and love. Jesus' words to "judge not" certainly do not forbid the practice of discipline, nor do they excuse our failures to be as discerning as we should be.

3. "If someone has been formally excluded from the church's fellowship, should they be allowed to attend worship and partake of the Lord's Supper?"

Opinions on this question vary widely. Many assume that offenders will naturally be excluded from public worship, while others assume they will be present, even that we should encourage them to attend. The reality is that, because worship services are something of a public event, it's difficult, if not impossible, to prevent anyone from attending.[3] (Naturally this would be different in a house church setting.) Laney points out that, even if we wanted to prohibit a disciplined member from attending worship, the attempt to evict someone would likely produce nothing more than embarrassment and a media event.[4] What's important isn't whether or not the disciplined person attends but what happens when he or she does so and what associations other members have with him or her outside the assembly.

---

[3] Historically speaking, many have advocated that disciplined people should be barred from the Lord's Supper, even if they attend worship. More recently, this is the position of Jonathan Leeman, although he fails to explain how this might be done (*Church Discipline*, 50).

[4] 58.

There could even be some positive advantages to the disciplined person's attending. It may be that the process of self-examination at the Lord's Supper and hearing the word of God preached will produce a willingness to repent.[5] Also the disciplined person's presence provides an opportunity for others to re-address the need for repentance, which previously has been ignored. If a disciplined person is present, this is certainly what should happen. Each time the person attends, they should be admonished concerning their need for repentance. Most likely if this happens each time the person attends, there either will be repentance or attendance will cease.

In my experience (and the experiences of those with whom I'm acquainted) this is seldom a real problem. Those who have been disciplined most often choose not to attend or may do so for a short time, then stop coming when they realize they will not experience the same fellowship they once enjoyed and will instead be admonished repeatedly to repent.

4. *"Should the church withdraw fellowship from people whose primary sin is that they have stopped attending worship?"*

Again, opinions differ widely. We must keep in mind that failing to attend worship is a symptom of far deeper spiritual troubles and should approach the problem from that perspective, as a symptom and not the disease itself. Something is clearly faulty with the discipleship of someone who voluntarily never assembles with the church. Also it should be the desire of every group of elders and of the church as a whole to keep track of every member and to be able to account for each one. Shepherding the flock would seem to require a knowledge of the whereabouts and spiritual status of the sheep.

---

[5] An exception to this would be cases where the disciplined person's presence would be divisive, that is, if they came to worship primarily to "campaign" for their cause or otherwise cause disruption in the assembly.

It seems therefore that, in the case of people who cease to attend worship and who will not respond to offers of pastoral counsel and guidance, some sort of disciplinary action is in order, if for no other reason than to bring to their attention the seriousness of consistently "missing church," as well as to keep the church informed of who is a member and who isn't. One of the important functions of church discipline is what sociologists call "boundary maintenance"—determining who is "in" and who is "out." This isn't the same as judging who is saved and who isn't, but it means demarcating in some sense who is living up to community expectations and who is not. The Scriptures spell out clearly the expected norms, including participation in worship (Heb 10.24–25). If someone consistently, over a long period of time and in spite of efforts to teach them the importance of worship, simply refuses to attend, something ought to be said to the church as a whole. This need not be a "delivering to Satan" but an informing of the congregation that this person is no longer attending and needs our prayers and admonitions to repent. The door is left open for them to return, but in the meantime the church realistically acknowledges that there is a problem. We shouldn't be shy about stating openly that it is wrong to stop attending worship, since to be silent could be construed as giving consent.

When careful, godly shepherding is taking place within a church, the elders will know who is chronically not attending and should be continually trying to discover the root cause of the problem and to persuade them to return. However, periodically (at least annually) it would be a good idea to make a formal attempt to reach out to such people and ask them if they wish to continue to be regarded as members or not. The results of such an inquiry can be numerous. Some will simply say no, they no longer desire to be associated with the church. Others, it will be discovered, will have begun attending elsewhere. Some won't respond at all. In any case, the church can be notified (perhaps by mail) of those who fail to respond or who indicate a disinterest in continuing as members of the local church. This will have the effect of letting everyone know who is and who is not to be considered part of the congregation. If someone is a member of the church, their membership should mean something to them, at least enough for them to attend worship or else explain why they aren't doing so. But we shouldn't simply allow non-attendance to go unacknowledged and uncorrected.

In short, no one should ever exit a church's fellowship, for whatever reason, without some sort of statement to that effect. A church which never acknowledged members who *moved* away would be doing a poor job of keeping track of its membership. One which never acknowledges that some have *fallen* away is doing worse.

5. "If someone withdraws their membership to avoid being disciplined by the church, is there anything left for the church to do, or does the individual's withdrawal end the matter?"

Some will argue that the church not only should not but *cannot* withdraw fellowship from someone who no longer attends or who has withdrawn their membership, since the person has "already withdrawn fellowship from the church" and "there is nothing left for the church to withdraw." However, it seems to me that such statements betray an inadequate understanding of fellowship and church membership. They imply that fellowship takes place only in our assemblies. In some cases this may actually be the situation, but in most it isn't. Many who practice sin habitually and/or stop attending worship continue to associate with other Christians in business and social situations. For the church to fail to go through with at least some form of disciplinary process when clearly called for, simply because someone has declared that he/she is no longer a member, would be a serious failure to recognize the true nature of fellowship and the realities of sin.

Even in situations where someone knows that disciplinary action is imminent and withdraws their membership to head it off, the church still needs to follow through so that members will know the offender's true status with the congregation. Otherwise they may continue to associate freely with someone with whom they should not. In such cases the announcement to the church would be different than in a situation involving a current member, but it should be done nonetheless. It could simply be stated that the person has chosen to withdraw their membership rather than face the discipline of the church. In such cases there would be no need to specify the nature of the sin, since to do so would accomplish nothing and might involve a violation of privacy laws.[6]

6. "How should the church's leaders go about 'telling it to the church' when someone has been resistant to efforts to lead them to repentance?"

Remember that in Matthew 18.15–18 Jesus said that a sinning believer should first be approached in private; then, if that fails, take one or two others with you; and, if that fails, "tell it to the church." The purpose is so that the entire congregation can become involved in trying to lead that person to repentance. This is a delicate and often-overlooked phase of congregational discipline that must be approached with great care. How and under what circumstances do we "tell it to the church"?

---

[6] In some cases where legal actions against churches have been effective, it has been because the church refused to acknowledge the changed status of a person who withdraws membership from the congregation. This changed status can be acknowledged, while at the same time letting the church know the person has left in order to avoid discipline. Such statements should, naturally, be carefully worded.

In the case of the incestuous man at Corinth, Paul offers one guideline regarding when discipline should occur: "When you are assembled in the name of the Lord Jesus and my spirit is present, with the power of our Lord Jesus, you are to deliver this man to Satan for the destruction of the flesh, so that his spirit may be saved in the day of the Lord" (1 Cor 5.4–5). "When you are assembled" seems to point to the normal Lord's Day worship assembly of the church. However, two factors need to be kept in mind.

First is the extreme nature of the form of discipline described in 1 Corinthians 5. It may be that Paul assumes that, in a situation so well known to the entire church (and perhaps to the outside community as well), nothing short of a public repudiation of sin will do. On the other hand, he might not have required a public announcement in cases of a less severe nature. We cannot know this for sure, since he doesn't say. Still, we must be cautious about treating all cases as though they were alike.

The second consideration is that "when you are assembled" could point to something other than the weekly worship assembly. It could have the sense of "when you are assembled to deal with this matter." In that case Paul would be thinking of a special called meeting for the express purpose of exposing someone's sins to the church.[7] Exactly when such a meeting would take place would depend on the decision of each church's leadership, and they would naturally encounter the difficulty that not all (maybe not even a majority) of the members will be present. A workable variation of this is to have the meeting at the close of morning worship (assuming that's the time when the most members will be present) after asking that all non-members excuse themselves. Since this would normally be a time for greeting visitors, a team of church leaders could be posted in the foyer to greet them as they

---

[7] Leeman (*Church Discipline*, 77) says that in his church "telling it to the church" is done in a private meeting "for members only."

leave and thank them for coming or engage them in conversation until the meeting concludes. The meeting need not be long, and members could soon join their guests afterward. While this may sound inappropriate to some (and it might be in some churches), non-members generally recognize that not everything that takes place within a church is necessarily their business and are unlikely to be offended if politely asked to allow the congregation a few minutes alone, as long as they are not simply left to find their own way out without being warmly greeted and welcomed as they leave. Often upon learning later what the meeting was about, visitors will express appreciation for the seriousness with which the church deals with sin. I'm sympathetic with the desire for our assemblies to be "visitor friendly," but this can be taken too far. The church doesn't assemble primarily for the benefit of visitors but in order to accomplish the will of God. Dealing adequately with sin in our midst must take precedence over impressing visitors.

It is sometimes suggested that "telling it to the church" can be accomplished by mail. While this might be an effective way of getting the information out to those we want to receive it, it detracts seriously from the fellowship aspect of the church coming together for discipline. Remember that Jesus' statement about "two or three being gathered together" was spoken in the context of coming together for discipline. This should be a time for collective prayer and of mourning over the sin in someone's life, sin that has brought the church to the point of needing to take such an exceptional action as telling it to the entire congregation.[8] A

---

[8] If the church is informed of someone's sin as part of worship, it would seem appropriate that the service should be geared toward lamentation and prayer. While most churches aren't very experienced at this form of worship, the "Psalms of Lament" suggest that it is at times appropriate. It would seem distinctly out of place to have a service filled with positive messages and upbeat singing, then to announce that a brother or sister's spiritual life is in such jeopardy as to require the intervention of the whole church and possibly even expulsion from the congregation.

letter, it seems to me, just doesn't have the same effect, but in some cases it might be a desirable way to inform the church.

7. *"When 'telling it to the church,' must the offender's sin be specified, or is it sufficient simply to say that the person has sinned?"*

The answer to this one depends on how one construes Jesus' admonition to "tell *it* to the church"; what is the "it"? If we take that to mean "tell the *situation*" (i.e., that someone is guilty of serious sin but without specifying the sin), then I suppose the sin might not need to be specified. On the other hand, it seems to me that the most natural understanding of "it" is the sin in question: "tell *the sin* to the church." Besides, it would be somewhat tricky to ask a church to participate in the disciplining of a fellow member (including urging them to repent) if they aren't even aware of the actual problem.

That said, I can envision situations in which telling the specific sin could be damaging to people other than the sinner or where a high degree of confidentiality needs to be maintained or where caution might need to be exercised for legal reasons (as in a pending legal action). In such a case, the church's leaders would be asking the congregation to trust them that the situation is as serious as they say it is and to encourage repentance without knowing the exact nature of the wrongdoing. This would likely be difficult to maintain over the entire process, however. An alternative approach to "telling it to the church" would be to inform the congregation publicly that a specific person has sinned and needs everyone's urging to repent and that those who wish to know more are welcome to meet with the elders, ministers, or others who may have been involved earlier in the process to discuss the specific reasons for the action being taken.

The concern here is, obviously, to spare embarrassment to the family of the one being disciplined or to others who might be involved (as in an instance of adultery or child molestation), as well as to spare embarrassment to the church as a whole. However, this is a situation where the church simply needs to face up to its responsibility, as unpleasant as it is. As for the offender's family (and perhaps close friends), they could be informed ahead of time when the public statement will be made and could make it a point to be absent from the meeting. Once again, however, the embarrassment for the family won't be limited to the announcement of disciplinary action; it will be in people knowing the sin itself, which will undoubtedly come out at some point anyway.

As I've stressed so often already, wise and prayerful leadership is the key to handling this question in the best possible way.

8. *"What should Christians do when a family member has been disciplined publicly? Should they continue to associate with them?"*

Suppose a woman's husband is disciplined by the church. Do her obligations to him as his wife come to an end? What about the relationship between adult children and their parents? Since Scripture offers no specific teachings to answer these questions, we must let conscience and prayerful consideration be our guide. It would seem that family obligations should not be sidestepped in such cases. A spouse, parent, or child could continue with normal family relations, it seems, while expressing their disapproval of the sin in the other person's life. This would not seem to be very different from living with a spouse who is not a Christian (1 Cor 7.12–13; 1 Pet 3.1–6). In cases of more distant relationships or where the offending family member is no longer a member of the same household (as in the case of adult children), the same avoidance could be practiced as with any other sinning Christian. There could be necessary exceptions to this, however, and we should be careful about passing judgment on people concerning their decisions regarding it.[9]

9. *"Should a church accept into its membership someone who has been disciplined by another congregation?"*

It sometimes happens that a Christian who has been publicly disciplined by Congregation A will simply go across town and become a member of Congregation B. Assuming that the leaders of Congregation B know the circumstances, should this person be accepted as a member? While some will argue that what happened at the previous church is "old business" and should be left behind, there is more here that needs to be considered.

First, it's very likely that the disciplining congregation has gone through a considerable amount of trauma in order to do what they should concerning a sinning member. For another church simply to disregard that and receive the person as a member anyway disparages their efforts and is likely to create resentment and possibly even a breach of fellowship between the two churches.

Second, if the person actually needed discipline but is allowed simply to walk away from it and be received elsewhere, the accepting church may be guilty of tacitly encouraging that person not to repent. No group of shepherds should take lightly such a burden of responsibility.

Third, it would serve the receiving congregation well to learn the nature of the offense for which the person was disciplined, since it might be something (false teaching, divisive attitude and/ or actions, etc.) that could have a detrimental effect in the new

---

[9] A possible exception to continued association with disciplined family members would be those who attempt to destroy the faith of their family members or whose moral influence is such that they simply need to be avoided. For a sensitively-written and well-researched discussion of this question in the larger context of apostasy, see J.R. Mackert, Jr., "A Response to Believing Family Members and Friends Regarding Laura" (unpublished manuscript, 2014. Available from the author at rod@rodmackert.com).

environment just as it did in the old. By doing so they may be able to avoid inviting trouble into their midst unnecessarily.

Naturally, it's impossible for church leaders to know the full story of everyone who presents themselves for membership, and it would be unwise indeed to try to determine everyone's fitness for membership. On the other hand, it's a good idea for churches to inquire whether or not a potential member left their former church home in good standing. Particularly if the new member is coming from a nearby church, it would be appropriate for the church's elders to meet with that person and ask why he or she felt the need to leave. If they discover that there was an unresolved disciplinary issue, there would be nothing wrong in refusing to receive that person into membership until the problem is resolved. Again, this may accomplish good on several fronts: encouraging repentance on the part of a habitual sinner, sparing the receiving congregation the agony of later problems, and enhancing relations with the church the disciplined person has left. Again, there are no hard-and-fast rules here, but wise leaders will take these things into consideration before accepting into membership someone who has been disciplined by another church.

I am aware that some churches feel the necessity to inform other churches in their community (at least those with whom they consider themselves to be in close fellowship) of any disciplinary action in order to head off the unwise reception of the disciplined person into membership. However, there are many pitfalls to this practice, and it would seem better to wait to be asked why someone left or to offer to meet with the leaders of any "Congregation B" that might be about to accept a disciplined person as a member.[10]

---

[10] Everett Ferguson offers good advice in this regard: "In a polity of congregational autonomy... disciplinary action pertains only to the local church, but each church will respect the decisions and action taken by a sister church. However, a different con-

10. *"Can one church withdraw its fellowship from a member of another congregation or from another congregation itself?"*

In considering this question it's important to observe that the context of *all* discipline described in the New Testament is the local church. Discipline is never an institutional process by which a multi-location organization passes sentence on someone's actions. Rather, it is always brothers and sisters within the local church approaching a sinning fellow member in order to seek to reclaim them for Christ.

When Jesus said "tell it to the church," He obviously didn't mean to the church at large in multiple locations. Likewise, Paul's instructions on discipline always come in the context of the needs and troubles of individual congregations where people know and care about one another. There is never a reaching beyond the local church to exercise discipline. While one congregation may limit its associations with another for a variety of reasons, proclaiming that "discipline" in a formal way to other churches is nowhere sanctioned in Scripture. Neither is it appropriate for a church to discipline someone in another congregation. That individual is part of a fellowship which has responsibility for him or her, and it is up to them to enact discipline whenever necessary. To attempt to do otherwise raises the question of the motives of those who wish to reach beyond their own sphere to discipline others. They should have more than enough to attend to by taking care of things at home.

11. *"How much time should be allowed for the disciplinary process from the time of first approaching the sinner to final withdrawal?"*

gregation in its autonomy is not bound by the decisions of another. That means that a person who feels a given church has acted unfairly has a 'court of appeal' by applying for membership in another congregation, which may then reconsider the merits of the action taken by another body of believers or reevaluate the events of long ago that appear differently in a new context" (*The Church of Christ*, 384–85).

Numerous factors affect the answer to this question.[11] First it should be noted that, since Jesus gave no time reference, this may not be something we should try to define too narrowly. At the same time, however, there are obvious pitfalls in sometimes acting either too slowly or too hastily.

As Jesus outlines the process of going to someone about their sin, sufficient time must be allowed to determine (a) if a sin actually has been or is being committed and (b) the attitude and intentions of the sinner. We shouldn't imagine that we can always go to someone and expect them to repent instantaneously. That may happen, but it may take some time for them to think about what has been brought to them to see how they will eventually respond. Once it is clearly established, however, that someone is guilty of sin and has no intention of repenting, the rest of the process need not take a great deal of time. Still, we should allow sufficient time for the testimony of the "one or two others" to have the desired effect, as well as a reasonable amount of time for the church to make its collective appeal.

However, there is an exception to what I've just said: If the situation is dangerous to the rest of the church, then there is a need to act sooner rather than later. That, I think, explains why Paul didn't instruct the Corinthians to go through "the steps" in dealing with the incestuous man in their midst. Such a shocking act of immorality was highly dangerous ("a little leaven leavens the whole lump of dough") and couldn't be allowed to continue. The same need for urgency might occur in cases of false teaching and/or divisiveness.

Another factor to consider is whether or not the church has been properly taught about discipline so as to be able to participate in it meaningfully. If not, it might be wise to take a sufficient amount of time to focus on this subject to bring the congregation up to speed so they will understand what must be done and their

---

[11] See the helpful discussion in Leeman, *Church Discipline*, 70–77.

role in it. However, this need not take months to accomplish if leaders make a diligent effort to do so. It may be necessary to put other things on hold in order to focus on this topic and the need for action. Ideally, of course, such teaching would be taking place periodically in every church so that there would be no exceptional need for it when a situation calls for discipline. Sadly, however, this is seldom the case.

As a general observation, it seems to me that the tendency of most churches and church leaders is to act too slowly rather than too quickly. Even situations of drastic immorality or falsehood are sometimes allowed to continue for years with nothing being done or said. When the subject finally comes up, someone is likely to say, "We don't want to act too hastily." The delay in carrying out discipline when it is sorely needed is simply an indication both of our lack of love for those overtaken in sin and of our lack of trust in the efficacy of the discipline which our Savior teaches us to enact.

Generally speaking, when we know of sin in someone's life, the time to act is now. There's usually very little to be gained (and sometimes much to be lost) by delaying.

12. *"Isn't withdrawing fellowship from someone likely to disrupt the overall aims and ministries of the congregation?"*

In a word, yes. And this is, I think, one of the primary reasons many church leaders prefer to not even think or talk about discipline. In churches where attendance is rising and ministries are growing, it's difficult to think about risking the negative effects of publicly disciplining someone. There's very little question that the discipline itself will distract attention from the day-to-day functioning of any church, and it's hard to think about doing anything that will have that effect. Why bring trouble on ourselves?

But here's the problem: If a church has among its members someone in need of discipline, *the "trouble" is already there, and we deceive ourselves if we think we can escape its effects by acting as though it doesn't exist.* Sooner or later it will catch up with us, and when it does the problems will be even larger than they are now. It's easy for us to lose sight of what the church is all about. We get so focused on our numerical growth, our budgets, our ministries and programs, and our reputation among other churches that we lose sight of the fact that first and foremost we are a family of believers serving our Lord and striving to help one another get to heaven. And when someone needs discipline in order to help him get there, what right do we have to ignore his plight and sacrifice him to our own goals and self-image? As I've emphasized repeatedly in this study, discipline is a matter of trust—and we display that trust by doing what the Lord teaches us to do.

So, yes, we may temporarily experience a set-back in the things we're trying to accomplish. Exercising discipline may even cost us some members, people who either don't understand or don't care about the meaning and purposes of discipline. But in the long run the church will be stronger and healthier when we simply do as Scripture so clearly teaches us to do.[12]

13. *"What is the potential impact of social media on church discipline, and how should church leaders take this into account?"*

As I've pointed out previously in this study, there is a need for confidentiality in order for discipline to have the desired effect,

---

[12] This is not to overlook the potentially positive effects of discipline, even in the short term. "There is a drawing power about a society in which there are clear distinctions between inside and out. Where there are standards it means something to be a member. Discipline, therefore, can be an aspect of evangelistic outreach... The disciplining of an erring member should be treated as another way of doing evangelism. Discipline is a way of offering the gospel and forgiveness to those who depart from the Christian lifestyle" (Ferguson, 389).

especially in the earlier stages of going to someone privately about their sin. Even later, however, if the matter has to be made known to the church at large, this ought to be considered a family matter and kept within the family. But in an age when some people feel the need to post online what they had for lunch or the fact that they have no particular plans for the next two hours, such confidentiality is extremely difficult to maintain. Likewise, some people simply have no filters about what is and isn't appropriate to post for all to see. So what can we do to help insure that discipline is dealt with confidentially? Here are a few suggestions how this might be accomplished.

First, church leaders would do well to emphasize in a general context (i.e., when not talking about the subject of discipline) that social media must be used with great caution. What the Bible teaches about gossip is just as true if it's done via the Internet as if it were done in person—and it's no less dangerous just because we don't see the people about whom or to whom we're talking. Simply because a medium of gossip is commonplace doesn't mean we shouldn't speak out against its abuse; in fact, it means we should speak out against it all the more.

Second, when we must tell someone's sin to the church, it is entirely appropriate and even necessary to emphasize to the entire church their responsibility to maintain confidentiality about the matter and the potential consequences of not doing so. It would be wise at this time to specify the need to avoid spreading word about this action via social media. Remember that posting everything they're aware of is so natural for some people that they might not even consider the potential for harm unless they are cautioned about it.

Third, misuse of media may itself require discipline. I have known of one church where a member disagreed violently with a decision made by the church's leaders. Rather than addressing this with them and/or with the rest of the congregation, she took to social media and slandered the church to virtually everyone she knew. In spite of the pleading of church leaders for her to stop, she refused and became even more virulent and un-Christian in her denunciations of her brothers in Christ. As a result, the church was on the brink of having to discipline her for her behavior, when someone finally made her see the damage she was causing, and she repented of it. I'm not suggesting that church leaders need to become media police, but when someone's abuse of social media becomes destructive to the church and its reputation, it needs to be stopped, and that may require the exercise of discipline.

No one who has ever done it would deny that practicing church discipline can be difficult. In fact, it can be one of the most heart-wrenching experiences in anyone's life. It requires all of the wisdom, love, and sensitivity we can muster to do it properly. But we cannot allow the difficulties involved or our unanswered questions to deter us from doing what Scripture clearly teaches is right. Surely the congregations to whom the apostles wrote experienced many of the same questions and anxieties that we do, and discipline was surely no less painful for them than for us. But they were commanded to take a stand against sin and for their fellow Christians, regardless of the difficulties involved. Only in this way can we hope to experience the spiritual health and holiness God intends us to enjoy, and only by trusting what Scripture teaches us about discipline can we enjoy God's fellowship and that of our brothers and sisters for all eternity.

For Thought and Discussion

1. What are the pros and cons of allowing a disfellowshiped person to attend worship?

2. In your opinion, can an individual Christian "withdraw fellowship from the church"? What should be the church's response when someone claims to have done this?

3. What suggestions can you offer concerning how a congregation can go about "telling it to the church" when a member requires congregational discipline? What do you think would be the most appropriate setting for this?

4. Explain in your own words why the practice of corrective church discipline isn't a violation of Matthew 7.1. Why do you think this verse is so often raised in objection to the practice of discipline?

5. What does your congregation normally do in the case of members who stop attending? Is the approach a biblical one, based on what you have learned from this study? Why or why not? What, if anything, do you think should be done differently?

6. How might the use of social media have a negative effect on the practice of church discipline? Can you think of ways it could be used for a positive effect in disciplinary situations?

7. How might a church go about preparing its members for the practice of church discipline? Has this topic been taught in the church you attend?

SEVENTEEN

What Now?

For the moment all discipline seems painful rather than pleas-
ant, but later it yields the peaceful fruit of righteousness to
those who have been trained by it. (Hebrews 12.11)

As this study comes to a close, my prayer is that your heart has
been moved to recognize the importance of discipline in order for
today's churches to be both healthy and holy—and not only to
recognize it but to be ready to do something about it, to put into
practice the things taught so clearly in Scripture. There's no question that a change of heart is what we so badly need in order for
discipline to become a common practice in the church once again.

In saying this, I realize that the practice of discipline has been
so far off the radar for most of us that the thought of actually doing it seems overwhelming. Our minds reel with thoughts and
fears of failure and dire consequences. What if we make a mistake? Will discipline really do any good, or will it only create confusion and do harm to the church? Won't people just be turned
off from the gospel if we act as drastically as the Bible says we
sometimes must in response to sin? What about lawsuits? Won't
we make the church look bad in the eyes of outsiders by practicing
something as archaic as church discipline? And even if we wanted
to, could we really do this lovingly and effectively?

So where do we begin? How do we overcome the inertia which in many churches has been building for generations? Assuming we are now convicted by God's word of the need for discipline, how do we get started?

There's no magic bullet for suddenly turning this situation around, but allow me to make a few suggestions.

Start with Confession and Repentance

We can take a cue from Scripture here, since quite often, when God's people got ready to take Him and His word seriously, they signaled their determination by acknowledging their past failures and their commitment to do better. Nehemiah 9 contains one such prayer of confession and repentance. In seeking to rededicate the rebuilt Temple and the city of Jerusalem, Nehemiah led the people in both hearing the words of God's law for a quarter of the day and confessing their sins for another quarter. Did you hear that? They confessed sin, not in a passing and generalized way, but for *hours*. There was no holding back, and we read such statements as "you have dealt faithfully and we have acted wickedly" (9.33) with many specific instances of their failures in spite of God's goodness interspersed throughout the lengthy prayer. Nehemiah knew that the city and its Temple worship could never be right until the *people* got right with God.

If we ever expect to have God's blessings in carrying out the discipline He requires, we must begin where Israel began, with confession of our sins in this regard and an open statement of our determination to do better. We must repent of our monumental failures to practice discipline on behalf of one another. Church leaders especially must acknowledge that our studied indifference to God's will is sin, that we have lost many more people to Satan than was necessary, that we've allowed our congregations to take sin less seriously than Scripture says we should, that we've not sought "the holiness without which no one will see the Lord" (Heb 12.14), and that we have been content with mere socializing rather than genuine fellowship in many of our churches.[1]

Our repentance must include the resolve to begin where we are and to do better. Often when church leaders begin to think about the need for discipline, they are so overwhelmed by past failures that they become paralyzed, as if it were too late to do any good. How do we begin to discipline when we have failed to do so for so long? Where do we start? Here's the answer: *Start with the people under your care right now.* It isn't possible to go back and correct the mistakes and omissions of the past, but you can resolve with God's help to do better with those you have now. A careless shepherd can't redeem lost sheep from the belly of the wolf, but he can be more vigilant with those he still has. To recognize our mistakes of the past but be paralyzed from doing better is incomplete repentance, and repentance must surely be the starting point.

While this kind of repentance needs to begin with church leaders, it isn't their responsibility alone. Individual Christians must develop the habit of being so concerned for one another's welfare that we simply can't ignore sin when it arises in someone's life. In some cases it may be necessary to "lead the leaders" in the right direction. All of us must acknowledge our responsibility for discipline, for this is where Scripture places the responsibility: squarely on the shoulders of the whole church.

Teach the Church

Confession and repentance may be the place to begin, but merely recognizing our failures of the past and resolving to do better won't move the church toward discipline. Many Christians are so lacking in understanding of this subject that it would be

---

[1] It should be noted that such a confession will have little effect unless it is acknowledged before the congregation, not just among its leaders.

disastrous to attempt to practice it without a period of thorough instruction. Not only do people need exposure to the Scriptures which speak of discipline specifically, but also to the supporting concepts of sin, holiness, and fellowship. From there we can proceed to the more specific aspects of discipline, such as how to confront lovingly about sin and what Scripture says about withholding or withdrawing fellowship whenever necessary.

Mark Littleton identifies five problems which make the practice of church discipline difficult:

1. *People wonder whether it will do any good.*

2. *No one is clear about what sins we are to discipline.*

3. *People fear the outcome.*

4. *People associate discipline with excommunication and intolerance.*

5. *People have few models of positive discipline to follow.*

In response he suggests five practices that create a healthy disciplinary environment:

1. *A clear understanding of sin and a desire for holiness.*

2. *Regarding church membership as a responsibility to love, admonish, and build one another up.*

3. *Practicing confession of sin on a personal level.*

4. *Teaching people how to admonish one another in love.*

5. *Follow-up and support for those who have sinned.*[2]

Obviously, most of Littleton's suggestions reflect a need for teaching, and not just about discipline but about what it means to be the church and the privilege and responsibility of being members of it. Our lack of discipline betrays a serious lack of understanding of who we are and what we are supposed to be about. Only careful, diligent teaching can correct this deficiency.

---

[2] Mark R. Littleton, "Church Discipline: A Remedy for What Ails the Body," *Christianity Today* (May 8, 1981): 30–33.

mber that Jesus' promise that "where two or three are gathered in my name, there am I among them" was spoken in the context of coming together to try to restore a sinning brother to the right way (Matt 18.15–20).

As for our fears that discipline will be a turn-off to those outside the church, we should rather be encouraged to believe that thoughtful outsiders will be turned on by a church which does more than just *talk* about sin and holiness. Let's face it: Our puny responses to God's instructions about discipline have betrayed a lack of faith, but if we will trust and obey, we will be amazed how He will bless us.

Our often-expressed fear of lawsuits says more than we care to admit about our attitude toward obedience to God. Especially since the case of the Collinsville, Oklahoma Church of Christ turned out so badly (from a financial point of view) for the church,[3] the vast majority of discussions of discipline have dealt with the legal aspects of it, mostly about how to avoid lawsuits. While this may be a legitimate concern, it should hardly be the church's *first* concern. *First and foremost we should be concerned about obeying God and about redeeming Christians who have strayed from the Spirit's way.* It may well be the case that churches will suffer financially or in other ways for practicing corrective discipline, but since when does that justify failure to obey? Where did we ever get the idea

---

[3] For the details see Laney, 127–139, and Yeakley, "Questions and Answers."

that the danger of suffering for righteousness' sake excuses us from practicing righteousness? Are we, as John White and Ken Blue suggest, more concerned about what is expedient than about what is right?[4] It's somewhat ironic that we've become so panicked over the legal question, since so few churches practice congregational discipline enough to be in any real danger.

J. Carl Laney tells a story about a little boy whose toy boat was blown far out of his reach into the pond where he was sailing it. Seeing his desperate attempts to retrieve it, an elderly gentleman came to help. Much to the little boy's horror, the old man began throwing rocks in the direction of the boat. But the boy soon saw the strategy. His friend threw the rocks beyond the boat so that the resulting ripples would drive it back toward shore. What had appeared to the boy to be a destructive action was actually just what was needed to accomplish his objective. In the same way, discipline may appear to us as destructive and counter-productive, but our Father knows what He's doing—and what we need to do. Trust Him.

Believe in the Positive Power of Discipline

Although most would acknowledge that God wouldn't teach us to do something useless or destructive to the church, our fears sometimes cause us to respond as if discipline were both useless and destructive. Much of our reasoning in this regard is simply false.

Take, for example, the often-heard complaint that practicing discipline will drive people away from the church. Nothing could be further from the truth. White and Blue rightly argue that people go away from the church not because of the practice of discipline but due to the lack of it. "Churches have become hospitals where sin-sick souls are given aspirin and entertainment

[4] White and Blue, 30.

to distract them from the diseases of their souls. God forgive us, we are more concerned with numbers than with holiness."[5] Joan Burge cites the example of St. Matthew Lutheran Church in Holt, Michigan, which practices discipline consistently. Members who stop attending and refuse counseling and restoration are declared to be "self-excommunicated." And in the 1970s the congregation grew from 100 to 1600 members in a span of only ten years.[6] I'm not suggesting that practicing discipline is the sole factor in such growth, but it obviously didn't hurt to any significant extent.

Francis Shaeffer observes that the lack of discipline has caused the church to lose power, purity, purpose, and integrity. He particularly enlarges on the last point: our witness to a skeptical world is severely damaged when all we do about sin is talk, while tolerating its presence in our midst.[7] If we will show the world that we take both sin and holiness seriously, we will regain the integrity which we have lost, and our efforts at evangelism will bear more fruit than we dare imagine.

But the positive power of discipline extends beyond our impact on the watching world. Taking a stand against sin in a more than merely verbal way will also produce stronger, healthier churches. Even if our efforts do not always produce the positive result of restoring erring sinners, they will still fortify the faith and commitment of those who remain faithful, and in a world where we are dangerously close to blending imperceptibly with the unbelieving world, what a tremendous blessing this would be. God gave us discipline to build us up, not tear us down. Use it!

---

[5] 34.

[6] Joan Burge, "The Church That Dares to Discipline," *Christian Life* (August, 1980, Vol. 42, No. 4): 26–27, 45–57. I have been unable to verify whether or not this church continues to practice this form of discipline. The information given was valid as of the time of publication of Burge's article in 1980.

[7] Francis A. Shaeffer, *The Church Before the Watching World* (Downers Grove, Illinois: InterVarsity Press, 1971), 62ff.

Develop Genuine Fellowship and Pastoral Care

As emphasized earlier in this book, discipline is an expression of fellowship and is the responsibility of all Christians. Churches who take discipline seriously must first take fellowship seriously and strive to build a closer body of believers in which all members accept the responsibility to watch out for one another's spiritual welfare and where going to one another about unconfessed sin is a natural expression of our love and concern. Until there is genuine fellowship, any attempts at discipline can only lead to disaster, as has so often been the case in the past. Where Christians have a negative view of discipline, often a leading cause is having experienced it outside the context of real, loving concern for the welfare of those disciplined. It isn't just something we do to "be biblical" but something we do because we care too much to let someone simply slip away from Christ and be lost. We must work hard to create a climate of love, trust, and interaction among our members. When we do, discipline will flow naturally out of this atmosphere of fellowship.

In order for this to happen, however, we need to restore genuine pastoral leadership in our churches. Churches must insist that elders truly shepherd the flock, not just make decisions, and should consider whether or not a man is likely to provide pastoral care to the entire church, including leading them in discipline when necessary. We need to appoint elders less for their business expertise and more for their shepherds' hearts. Such men will lead the way and set the example of genuine love and concern for one another, and the result will be a transformed fellowship among church members. As I hope you can see by now, restoring the practice of church discipline means restoring more than just one ancient Christian practice; it means restoring some fundamental characteristics of the church which have long been lacking.

Make Holiness Our Priority

To both Israel and the church, God has said, "You shall be holy, for I am holy" (Lev 11.44; 1 Pet 1.16). Our behavior is to reflect in every way the character and nature of God, "the Holy One of Israel." The bottom line of discipline is whether or not we are serious about pleasing God and reflecting His character in our own. To accomplish that, we must wake up from our entertainment, comfort-oriented mentality and get back to talking about being God's holy people, with all that such holiness involves. But we must do more than simply talk. We must teach holiness, practice holiness, and discipline those who refuse the holy conduct to which God has called us. Remember that God "disciplines us for our good, that we may share his holiness" (Heb 12.10) and that without holiness "no one will see the Lord" (Heb 12.14). Partaking in God's holiness should be the primary aim of each of our lives, and we must recognize the essential role of discipline in that sanctification process. God disciplines us for our good. We must discipline ourselves for our good. And we must discipline one another, for the good of everyone in the body and for the glory of God.

For Thought and Discussion

1. Which of the suggestions for beginning the practice of discipline discussed in this chapter is a strong-point of your congregation? In which of these is the church where you worship most lacking? What can be done to improve this situation?

2. Can you think of Bible examples of people who were called upon to do what seemed unreasonable and potentially destructive yet were blessed by God for going ahead in faith?

3. How might your congregation be different if discipline were practiced consistently? Do you think you would find it a more attractive and spiritually helpful place, or less so? Why?

4. Read Acts 5.1–14. What effect did God's discipline of Ananias and Sapphira have on the rest of the Jerusalem church? On those outside the church? What bearing, if any, does this have on the need for congregational discipline today?

5. What can you do personally to make holiness more of a priority in your own life? In the congregation where you worship?

Summary

Key Thoughts from the Study of Corrective Church Discipline

1. Discipline has always been part of God's will for His people, including for the church today.

2. Corrective church discipline is not a burden God has placed upon the church, but rather a gift for helping us to be healthier and holier.

3. The primary goals of corrective discipline are (a) to retain or regain an offender within the church's fellowship and (b) to protect the church from unwholesome influences.

4. In spite of an abundance of New Testament teaching, churches today are largely negligent in the practice of corrective discipline, which is nothing less than disobedience.

5. Our negligence in the practice of discipline is due primarily to (a) lack of trust in what God has told us to do, (b) lack of sufficient love for those who are overtaken by sin, and (c) a tendency to accommodate ourselves to a permissive pluralistic society.

6. It is no more unloving for us to discipline one another than it is for God to discipline us.

7. Discipline is important for maintaining the boundaries between God's sanctified people and the world which does not acknowledge Him. This is as important for the church as for any other family.

8. Congregational discipline can only be exercised in the context of genuine fellowship and concern for one another. Apart from such fellowship, it is more likely to be destructive than constructive.

9. Church discipline begins when one Christian approaches another concerning sin in his or her life. From there the circle of those involved must be limited as much as possible. Confidentiality is critical in the early stages.

10. Rather than providing a "one-size-fits-all" sequence of steps for every situation requiring discipline, the New Testament provides a variety of means by which we can effectively correct one another, so that we can fit the action to the specific needs of the situation.

11. Withdrawal of the church's fellowship is the most extreme form of corrective discipline and should only be used when absolutely necessary.

12. Even the withdrawal of fellowship is not the final act of discipline; we must always stand ready to extend forgiveness to those who repent.

13. The practice of church discipline will spare churches from the destructive activities and teachings of misguided people.

14. Church discipline is the responsibility of every Christian, since the New Testament texts are directed to all believers, but church leaders have a critical role to play in the exercise of discipline, since churches most often will not engage in discipline unless they are led to do so.

15. We need a re-definition of the role of elders which includes their leading the church in discipline whenever necessary.

16. Rather than repelling outsiders, discipline will attract many who will respect the fact that the church takes sin seriously.

Also by Tommy South

Uncommon Sense
The Wisdom of James for Dispossessed Believers

Wisdom is the dominant theme of James' letter-and it is difficult to imagine a greater or more important theme for readers today who live in a world that seems almost totally devoid of wisdom. Throughout the history of our country, Christians have enjoyed a majority status and the deference that goes with it, but that circumstance has changed dramatically in recent years. Being a Christian has shifted from being an asset to being a liability (socially speaking), with many associating our faith with bigotry, hypocrisy, and a judgmental spirit-and the situation doesn't seem likely to change in the foreseeable future. This means that Christians must learn to live according to our marginalized status and to do so with all the wisdom God supplies, so that we not only hold firmly to our convictions but do so in a manner that causes others to see Jesus in us in spite of their prejudices. That's what it means to be dispossessed, and it is why James' message is so vital for our times. 181 pages, $12.99 (PB).

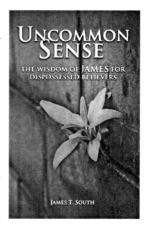

Also by Tommy South

Just Jesus
The Evidence of History

Few people are able to ignore Jesus. He has devotees and detractors, but hardly anyone is neutral about him. But how much do we know about him? Whether we love him or loathe him, it only makes sense that we know what and whom we're talking about. *Just Jesus* is about what we can know about Jesus. Jesus isn't just a religious idea but a phenomenon of history. That means we can and should ask about him all of the historical  questions we can think of and see which ones can and can't be answered. Fortunately, we're able to learn a lot more about Jesus than most people think. 152 pages, $9.99 (PB).